First
the Antichrist

Also by the Author
The Church and the Tribulation
Mark: A Commentary on His Apology for the Cross
*Matthew: A Commentary on His Handbook for a Mixed
  Church under Persecution*
Soma in Biblical Theology . . .
A Survey of the New Testament
The Use of the Old Testament in St. Matthew's Gospel . . .

First
the Antichrist

*A Book for Lay Christians
Approaching the Third Millennium
and Inquiring Whether Jesus Will Come
to Take the Church out of the World
before the Tribulation*

Bob Gundry

Baker Books
A Division of Baker Book House Co
Grand Rapids, Michigan 49516

© 1997 by Bob Gundry

Published by Baker Books
a division of Baker Book House Company
P.O. Box 6287, Grand Rapids, MI 49516-6287

Printed in the United States of America

ISBN: 0-8010-5764-7

Library of Congress Cataloging-in-Publication Data is on file at the Library of Congress, Washington, D.C.

For information about academic books, resources for Christian leaders, and all new releases available from Baker Book House, visit our web site:
http://www.bakerbooks.com/

CONTENTS

PREFACE

This book comes in response to numerous requests now that an earlier and more technical book of mine on the same topic has long been out of print and out of stock. Those who have read the earlier book (*The Church and the Tribulation* [Grand Rapids: Zondervan, 1973]) will notice some new arguments and a different interpretation here and there, but no fundamental change. The present book inclines toward a different audience than the earlier one did, however—lay people as distinguished from experts—and adapts its style to this audience as well as its argument to discussions that have taken place during the intervening years. Yet experts, too, will need to read the updated argument, and the postscript concerning Pseudo-Ephraem speaks quite directly to experts about a brandnew point at issue. For those desirous of tracking down materials related to Pseudo-Ephraem, I've supplied numerous references in parentheses and notes. On the other hand, each chapter ends with a sidebar, often quite extended, which adds details that might have been treated in ponderous notes or appendixes.

Bob Gundry
Westmont College

Setting Up   1

Antichrist is coming. Many antichrists have already come, to be sure. But we're talking *serious* antichrist—*the* Antichrist. Nearly an incarnation of the Devil himself.

The Coming of Antichrist

This Antichrist will arrive during the tribulation. The world and various people in it have suffered many tribulations, of course. But again, we're talking *serious* tribulation—*the* tribulation. A period of several years dominated by the Antichrist and characterized by horrors and suffering of unprecedented severity and extent. Also a period when God will once again concentrate his attention on the nation of Israel.

The Tribulation as Antichrist's Time

But the Christian church, at least that part of it which can truly be called Christian, is looking for the coming of Christ. So he must be coming back before the tribulation. Otherwise the church would be looking for the coming of the Antichrist instead of Christ's coming. Yet Christ can't stay here when he comes back before the tribulation. If he did stay here, the tribulation couldn't take place. He must come back, then, just close enough to grab Christians

Christ's Coming to Take the Church out of the World

out of the world and take them with him to heaven for reward and celebration while tribulation overwhelms the earth.

Taking the Church along with the Holy Spirit

In the meantime, though, the presence of the Holy Spirit on earth keeps the Antichrist from making his appearance. Not until the Holy Spirit is taken away will the Antichrist be able to appear. Since the Holy Spirit presently resides in the church, the taking of the Holy Spirit from earth carries with it the taking of the church from earth, too. You can't have the church without the Holy Spirit.

Exemption

As a result of being grabbed out of the world by Christ and taken away with the Holy Spirit, the church won't have to suffer any of those horrors that people left on earth will have to suffer. Nor will the church have to face the Antichrist. Best of all, the church won't be exposed to God's wrath, poured out on earth during the tribulation, or even live here during that terrible time. More than mere protection—complete removal!

Conversions during the Tribulation

Of course, the sudden removal of all true Christians won't go unnoticed. So despite deceptions practiced on people by the Antichrist, many of those people will convert to Christ. Among the ones who do will be 144,000 of the people of Israel. They will turn into evangelists, filling the vacuum of Christian witness left by removal of the church.

Christ's Coming with the Church to Establish His Kingdom on Earth

After the tribulation has run its course, the church will accompany Christ on his return to earth. This time he'll come all the way down to establish his kingdom. The Christians who make up the church will have already gotten their glorified bodies. They'll have gotten them when at Jesus' coming before the tribulation he raised de-

ceased Christians from the dead and translated into immortal bodies the mortal bodies
of Christians still living at the time. So people who didn't convert until the tribulation,
and thus had missed the earlier resurrection
and translation, will pass right into the
earthly kingdom of Christ with their mortal
bodies intact. They'll have children and
grandchildren and "replenish the earth."
The earth would sure seem to need replen-
ishing, what with all the death and destruction and divine judgment of the wicked that
took place during the tribulation and at
Christ's coming just afterward.

It all makes sense, doesn't it? Just as the
New Testament divides the Messiah's
seemingly single coming, as predicted in
the Old Testament, into two comings, one
before the age of the church and a later
one, so we should divide the second coming in two, a coming *for* the church before
the tribulation and a coming *with* the
church after the tribulation.

Dividing the Second Coming

SIDEBAR

Biblical Sense

The scenario that has just been set up
may make sense, but all Bible-believing
Christians agree that making sense isn't the
most important thing. More important is
what the Bible teaches. Better yet, what the
Bible teaches determines what makes sense.
So we need to see, not whether the scenario
makes sense in and of itself, but whether it
makes sense *of the Bible*. That should be a
profitable exercise, maybe even an exciting
one. It will certainly be educational. But first
we need to canvass the Christian world for
the popularity of this scenario.

CANVASSING   2

The preceding scenario: there's something odd about its history. Not for about seventeen hundred years did anybody imagine it's what the Bible teaches. Then a belief that it *is* what the Bible teaches attained some popularity in Great Britain. But there, very few Christians believe it anymore. I mean evangelical Christians, people who really do believe in the second coming of Jesus Christ.

Great Britain

Even in the United States, to which the belief spread during the late 1800s, fewer and fewer evangelical Christian theologians and Bible scholars are teaching a return of Jesus before the tribulation. Not because they've stopped believing the Bible. They wouldn't be evangelical if they had. Rather, they just don't find good biblical, theological evidence for the scenario, and they find much against it.

The United States

In fact, the scenario has become something of an embarrassment. Even at educational institutions where you'd expect to find strong support—seminaries and colleges traditionally dubbed "dispensational-

Seminaries and Colleges

13

ist"—you can detect a lot less enthusiasm than there used to be, and hear some privately stated wishing that the requirement of believing in a pretrib rapture (as it is called) would go away. Teachers at these institutions have told me so. They've told others as well. The scenario has become too hard to defend. It hasn't stood up to criticism from Bible-believing scholars.

Time-Lag   But changing a doctrinal standard is risky. Boards of trustees consist mainly of nonscholars and nontheologians. They're naturally wary, sometimes with good reason. And it's hard to tell church members that they've been taught wrongly all their lives. What would happen to pastors' credibility? No wonder there's a time-lag between what's happening in the world of biblical and theological scholarship and the thinking of lay people. You get similar time-lags in other fields (science, art, music, literature, etc.).

Historical Insignificance   As for nonevangelicals, many of them don't even know about the existence of a belief that Jesus will come back to evacuate the church before an unprecedented tribulation strikes the world. Some of these nonevangelicals, especially the scholars among them, know a great deal about the Bible, theology, and history. But they don't know about this belief. That's how small a blip it is on the wide screen of various beliefs held by Christians throughout the centuries. The belief retains its popularity mainly at the clerical and lay levels of certain circles in American evangelicalism and on mission fields to which these circles have exported it.

Wishful Thinking   Those nonevangelicals who do know about the belief regard it as a curiosity, because it looks to them very far off-base from what the Bible really teaches—whether or not they themselves accept that teaching— and because it looks to them like the wishful thinking of some upwardly mobile Christians who want a crown without a cross and who, despite their confessing the Bible to be God's very Word, eagerly if not consciously accept a bending of its meaning to match the comfort of their lifestyle. As a pretrib friend candidly admitted to me about the possibility of going through the tribulation, "Who wants to be made into hamburger?" I was also once told that when a well-known teacher of Bible prophecy described the tribulation in gruesome detail and then exclaimed, "But the church won't be here!" the whole audience—a large one—burst into applause. Is something wrong here?

Just as many nonevangelicals don't know anything about pretribulationism, I grew up as an evangelical who didn't know anything *except* pretribulationism. At first I didn't even know of a disagreement on the topic. Later I heard dark rumors that some Christians don't believe in a coming of Jesus before the tribulation—but they must be straying dangerously from the Bible and standard Christian doctrine. Or so I was told, and so I thought.

A Bit of Autobiography

I enrolled in a college. It was Christian. My teachers fed me the expected pretribulational fare, with an academic flavor added. I still respect those teachers. By and large they were good, very good, but somehow the suspicion grew on me that their teaching on this topic didn't sit so easily with biblical texts as their other

First Impressions

teaching did. So I decided to erase from my mind as far as was humanly possible everything I'd heard and read about the second coming, to read through the entire New Testament afresh, pay special attention to passages dealing with the tribulation and Jesus' return, and see what first impressions might be. They were that he is *not* said to return before the tribulation, but only afterwards. (Everybody who believes in a future period of special tribulation agrees that Jesus will return afterwards, so a preliminary coming is the only one in question.)

Confirmation Those first impressions were so disturbing that I repeated the exercise, only to have the impressions confirmed. Talking with my teachers and fellow students failed to turn up any convincing evidence to the contrary. Neither did reading reams of pretrib literature, both popular and scholarly. I still hadn't heard or read so much as a single sentence of argument for any view other than pretribulationism. Only then did I begin to read some literature taking a different tack, and to discover in that literature what had already become plain enough to me in the Bible itself, and to discover as well that throughout history the vast majority of Christians have never thought of a pretrib rapture.

Interpretation versus Imposition Other people tell similar stories. But these stories carry conviction only for us who tell them. How about the general run of Christians nowadays? On the one side, they have the good sense to recognize a difference between teaching that grows out of Scripture and teaching that is forced on it, and they want to know the truth of biblical teaching about Jesus' return. But they don't have the time or training for advanced study of this topic.

On the other side, the approach of a new millennium, the establishment of The Pre-Trib Research Center in Washington, D.C., to "prove to preachers and lay people alike" that belief in a pretrib rapture "is indeed biblical" and "of central importance" because "the New Testament places it as the central heartthrob of motivation for Christians," and "to help, and in a sense, restore and strengthen the teaching of the Pre-Trib rapture" with newsletters, books, booklets, papers, audio- and videocassettes, a prophecy cassette club, and conferences,[1] and the increasing use of TV and other mass media by Bible prophecy hucksters (not that all or only teachers of pretribulationism deserve this epithet, but a number of them do)—all these developments are exposing the laity to a popular upsurge in predictions of a soon-coming tribulation for the world, and to an equally popular upsurge in promises of prior evacuation for Christians. Offering a sad example of this phenomenon is the shamelessly maudlin appeal to escapism in the rhetorical question asked by the head of The Pre-Trib Research Center: "Are you able to look at your children playing in the sunlight and believe firmly in your heart that they will not have to endure the monstrous horrors of the Tribulation?"[2]

Pretrib Research and Development

1. Tim LaHaye and Tommy Ice, "The Pre-Trib Research Center: A New Beginning," *Pre-Trib Perspectives* 1/1 (May 1994): 2.
2. Tim LaHaye, *No Fear of the Storm* (Sisters, Oreg.: Multnomah, 1992), 14.

**Scandal
and Scripture**

The time-lag separating the bulk of biblical and theological scholarship from lay people has stretched out too long. What's merely embarrassing now threatens to become downright scandalous by the turn of the millennium. So where do we go from here? To the Bible, of course. It's our first, last, and highest court of appeal. Let's play catch-up.

SIDEBAR

**Recognizing
a Trend**

When my more technical critique of the pretrib theory was published over twenty years ago, the acknowledged dean of pretribulationists, Dr. John F. Walvoord, instituted a new course at Dallas Theological Seminary to counteract the obviously growing trend away from pretribulationism. Some students who took the course found it unintentionally convincing of pretribulationism's biblical and theological bankruptcy. So I was told from within the class without solicitation and without previous acquaintance. This incident is representative of what has been happening in academic circles for some decades now but has not filtered through to very many lay Christians.[3]

3. A point-by-point refutation of Walvoord's *The Blessed Hope and the Tribulation* (Grand Rapids: Zondervan, 1976), which he wrote almost entirely in reaction against my *Church and the Tribulation*, is available from me for $5 at 955 La Paz Road, Santa Barbara, CA 93108-1099. The refutation runs to about 23,000 words, including an appendix that deals with a review of my book by Charles C. Ryrie in *Bibliotheca Sacra* 131 (1974): 173–79.

WATCHING 3

But how can I watch for the second coming, as the New Testament tells me to do, if Jesus won't return till after the tribulation? That's usually the first question asked by people who've been taught that Jesus will return for them before the tribulation, and then are told that what they've been taught is wrong. Of course, the New Testament does tell Christians to watch for the second coming. Nobody disputes that fact. What kind of watching is the New Testament talking about, though? And what coming of Jesus does it say to watch for?

Christians' Watching and Christ's Returning

The Apostle Paul tells Christians in the church at Thessalonica, Greece, that they should be watchful for the coming of "the Day of the Lord" (1 Thess. 5:1–11, especially verse 6: "Therefore, then, let us not sleep, as the rest do, but let us watch and stay sober"). Paul has just described "the coming of the Lord," which includes a catching up, or rapture, of Christians "to meet the Lord in the air" as he descends (1 Thess. 4:16–17). So in context the Day of the Lord

Watching for the Day of the Lord as the Day of His Coming

is the day of his coming and of Christians' meeting him then.

As a Thief on Unsaved People But Not on Christians

Also included are statements that the Day of the Lord will come on unsaved people ("them") "as a thief at night," but that it will *not* overtake Christians that way ("But you, brothers and sisters, are not in darkness that the day should overtake you as a thief" [1 Thess. 5:2–4]). Why not?

Hardly because it won't overtake them at all, for then "as a thief" would lose its point. Rather, because Christians are "not in darkness" (verse 4). They don't need instruction on "the times and seasons" (verse 1). They already know whose coming has to precede the Lord's coming, for Paul told them when he was with them in person (2 Thess. 2:5).

Antichrist's Coming before Christ Comes

And whose coming will that be? The Antichrist's. Paul calls him "the man of lawlessness," more commonly known to us as "the Antichrist" (1 John 2:18; 4:3) or "the Beast" (Rev. 13:1–18), and Paul says not only that "the Day of the Lord" won't arrive unless that evil figure "is revealed" but also that "the rebellion" which he will lead against all divinity except his own (claimed falsely, of course) "comes first" (2 Thess. 2:1–4).

Antichrist's Rebellion, Not Christians' Departure

The word translated "rebellion" is sometimes translated "apostasy"—or even "departure," as though it refers to a rapture of the church that will take place before the Day of the Lord arrives. But you have to wonder why Paul would tell Christians to be watchful for the Day of the Lord if they're going to depart from the world before that day arrives. Besides, by New Testament times the noun has advanced beyond the notion of simple departure of a spatial kind and has acquired the special connotation of a political or religious departure, that is, rebellion or apostasy.

The next point isn't essential, but since Paul gives no indication that the man of lawlessness, the Antichrist, will ever have professed allegiance to God and Christ, "rebellion" seems a better translation than "apostasy," which would imply an earlier such allegiance. Paul defines the rebellion in terms of the Antichrist's "opposing and exalting himself above everyone called God or object of worship, so that he sits in God's temple making himself out to be God" (verse 4).

Exclusion of the Tribulation from the Day of the Lord

When will this rebellion take place? During the tribulation, as agreed by everybody who believes in a future, unprecedented tribulation (see especially Rev. 13:1–18; also Matt. 24:29–31 on the futurity of the tribulation inasmuch as the second coming is said to occur "immediately after" the tribulation but hasn't yet occurred, nor have the events recognizably unique to the tribulation occurred). So the Day of the Lord can't arrive till after the rebellion that Antichrist will lead during the tribulation, a rebellion that will then reveal him for who he really is (thus the mention of his rebellion before his revelation). Yet Christians are supposed to watch for that posttribulational day. It doesn't make sense to watch for it if you're going to be removed from the scene years ahead of time. (The tribulation is usually figured at seven years—see Dan. 9:24–27 with the division into half of seven years at Dan. 7:25; 12:7; Rev. 11:2–3; 12:6, 14; 13:5).

No Division of the Day of the Lord

Pretribulational attempts to distinguish different days of the Lord, or to divide the Day of the Lord into different segments, and to say that Paul talks about one day or segment in 1 Thessalonians and about another day or segment in 2 Thessalonians— these attempts only betray a desperation to evade the plain sense of Paul's statements, and they turn those statements into a confusing mishmash that discredits the clarity and truth of Scripture. For if the rapture occurs before the tribulation and the tribulation makes up the first segment of the Day of the Lord, Paul's statement that the Day of the Lord can't come unless the Antichrist's rebellion and revelation come first is misleading to the point of falsehood.

Pretrib Irrelevance

It is also irrelevant, at least to Christians such as Paul's Thessalonian audience. For a pretrib Paul should have told them that the Day of the Lord won't come unless *the rapture* comes first. The coming first of the Antichrist's rebellion and revelation wouldn't matter to Christians if they won't be here anyway. And if, on the other hand, pretribulationism is true and the Day of the Lord doesn't start till after the tribulation, Paul's statement that that day won't come till the Antichrist's rebellion and revelation come first—this statement is satisfied but the command to watch for the Day of the Lord becomes misleading as well as irrelevant.

Watching for a Posttrib Day

So first the Antichrist. Only then the Christ. First the tribulation. Only then the Day of the Lord. Christians aren't in the dark. They won't be surprised by the Day of the Lord, the coming of Christ. They'll know ahead of time that the Antichrist's rebellion and revelation signal its nearness. What are Christians to watch for, then? A day and a coming that follow the tribulation. And what kind of watching are Christians to practice? A watching that takes account of events known by them to precede and signal the event watched for. It just isn't true what teachers of pretribulationism often say—that for Christians, watching is never connected with events that will take place beforehand in the tribulation. Paul makes this connection close and explicit.

How do Paul's kind and object of watching match up with those of Jesus? Couldn't do better. "When you see these things taking place [Jesus has just been describing events in the tribulation], know that he is near, at the doors [he has also just been describing the second coming, which he puts 'after that tribulation']" (Mark 13:29 with 13:18–28, especially verses 19, 24–26). Saying the same thing in only slightly different phraseology are Matthew 24:33 with 24:2–30 and Luke 21:31 with 21:23b–27, 29–30. Luke 21:28 quotes Jesus differently but to the same effect: "Now as these things are beginning to happen, stand erect and lift up your heads, because your redemption is coming near." Again, he has just described the second coming.

Watching through the Trib according to Jesus

Nowhere in these passages do we find any description of a preliminary coming of Jesus before the tribulation. He describes only his coming afterwards and puts his commands to watch in direct connection with that coming, not an earlier one. And, like Paul, he puts watching in terms of recognizing prior events that signal the nearness of the event watched for, not in terms of readiness for an event that could happen at any moment because nothing known has to happen beforehand (as pretribulation-ism would have people believe).

Watching for a Posttrib Coming according to Revelation

Revelation 16:15 corresponds. There Jesus talks again about his coming "as a thief" (compare the coming of the Day of the Lord "as a thief at night") and pro-nounces a blessing on the person "watch-ing" for it. He makes these statements in the middle of a description of the sixth bowl of God's wrath, poured out at the end of the tribulation. For the seven bowls are filled with "the seven last plagues" representing "the wrath of God" (Rev. 15:1, 7; 16:1). Moreover, the sixth bowl deals with prepa-rations for the Battle of Armageddon (Rev. 16:12–14, 16), which takes place at the com-ing of Christ after the tribulation (Rev. 17:14; 19:11–21). And as a whole, the Book of Revelation is addressed to churches (1:4), so that this watching has to do with Christians in relation to events of the tribu-lation and the second coming following it.

Watching for Events That Can't Happen at Any Moment

None of this evidence should surprise us. The various verbs used in watching for Jesus' return are elsewhere used in watching not only for events that can take place at any moment but also for events that can't. One of those verbs, for example, refers to watching for the resurrection of the unrighteous (Acts 24:15), which pretrib teachers themselves put more than a thousand years in the future (Rev. 20:1–15), and to watching for the mar-riageable age of sons that aren't even born yet (Ruth 1:13 in the Septuagint, a Greek translation of the Old Testament that is often quoted in the New Testament). An-other such verb refers to watching for

Noah's flood during a period known to last 120 years before that event could take place (1 Peter 3:20 with Gen. 6:3). Another refers to watching for new heavens and the new earth, which everybody agrees will not come into being at least till after the tribulation puts the old heavens and old earth through their death throes (2 Peter 3:13), and perhaps or probably not till after the further thousand years of Christ's millennial rule (Revelation 20–22).

Yet another verb compares Christians' watching for the return of Jesus to farmers' watching patiently for a harvest that can arrive only after the prolonged period of early and latter rains (James 5:7). Two other verbs refer to watching for the dawn, hardly the sort of event that can happen at any moment the way pretribulationism says the church's rapture can (3 Maccabees 5:24; Homer *Odyssey* 19.342). And so on. A couple of the verbs, one of them the most commonly used of all in relation to the second coming, mean to watch simply in the sense of keeping awake or alert, as in prayer (Matt. 26:38, 40, 41; Mark 14:34, 37, 38; Eph. 6:18; Col. 4:2).

In itself, then, watching doesn't tell us that Jesus might come back, much less *must* come back, before the tribulation else we wouldn't need to watch for his coming. Factors in the context determine whether watching means looking for an event that might happen before any other event that you know about has to happen, or looking for an event that can't happen till other events happen that you know about. As we've seen, factors in the context of watching for Jesus' return point to watching for an event that can't take place till other fore-known events—those of the tribulation—take place.

Other Events Known to Precede the Second Coming

In addition to the tribulation, there are other indications of known delays in the second coming. Carrying out the Great Commission required such a delay (Matt. 28:18–20; Luke 24:47–48; Acts 1:8; 22:21—note especially the phrases "all the nations," "to the end of the earth," "far away to the Gentiles," and their implication of delay). So also did Jesus' prediction that Peter would die at an infirm old age (John 21:18–19; 2 Peter 1:14). If these known delays didn't kill the expectancy of early Christians who knew about them, neither does a delay caused by the tribulation need to kill the expectancy of Christians who know about that delay and live at the end of the age. Matthew 24:45–51 and Luke 12:41–48 condemn taking selfish advantage of a delay, not the recognition of one: "But if that evil servant should say in his heart, 'My master is delaying,' and should begin to beat his fellow servants and should eat and drink with the drunkards [and so on]."

Knowing the Nearness but not the Day or Hour because of a Shortening

Doesn't Jesus say that "no one knows the day or the hour" of his coming, though (Matt. 24:36; Mark 13:32; compare Matt. 24:42–25:13; Mark 13:33–37; Acts 1:7)? Yes, he does. If Christians are to enter the tribulation, then, couldn't they count seven years to the end, or at least three and a half years to the end from "the abomination of desolation" in the middle, and by such simple arithmetic come to know the time of Jesus' coming and thus not need to watch alertly? No, they couldn't, because he also says that "those days [of 'great tribulation'] will be cut off" (Matt. 24:21–22; similarly Mark 13:19–20). "For the elect's sake," in other words, God won't allow the seven years of tribulation to run their full course. How much he will cut off nobody knows, and therefore nobody knows the exact time of Jesus' return ("the day or the hour"), though all alert and knowledgeable Christians will know from the events of the tribulation that "he is near, at the doors." We shouldn't forget that he makes his statement about not knowing the day or the hour, just as he issues the commands to watch, in immediate connection with his coming *after* the tribulation.

Revelation 10:1–4 backs up what Jesus says. There, "the seven thunders uttered their sounds." Apparently the seven thunders consist of various tribulational plagues, as do the seven seals, the seven trumpets, and the seven bowls among which the seven thunders are mentioned. But we read no description of plagues under the seven thunders as we do under the other series of seven. Instead, we read that when John the seer is about to write down the seven thunders, a voice from heaven tells him to seal them up.

Shortening the Trib by Cancelling the Seven Thunders

Now *un*sealing the seven seals caused the plagues under them to take place—not merely to be revealed by predictive prophecy, but to *take place* (in the prophetic future of a vision, of course—see Rev. 6:1, 3, 5, 7, 9, 12; 8:1). So sealing *up* the seven thunders, the opposite of unsealing them, causes them *not* to take place. They're cancelled, with the result that—to borrow the words of Jesus—"those days" of "great tribulation" are "cut off" and nobody knows the exact time, "the day or the hour," of his subsequent coming, though it's obvious from the plagues of seals, trumpets, and bowls and from the rebellion and revelation of the Antichrist that Jesus is going to return soon.

Incentives for Holy Living

Does such a small amount of temporal uncertainty salvage the incentive for holy living that "the blessed hope" of Jesus' return is supposed to provide (Titus 2:11–14; 2 Peter 3:10–14; 1 John 3:1–3)? No salvage job is needed. It's not a coming of Christ before the tribulation that motivates the church to live holy; rather, "the grace of God" (Titus 2:11–14), the "burning up" of the old creation and "promise" of "new heavens and a new earth in which righteousness dwells" (2 Peter 3:10–14), and the expectation of being "like him [Jesus] when he appears," whenever he does (1 John 3:1–3). Besides, we'll not be judged solely for what we happen to be doing at the moment of his coming. Our whole life will pass in review before him. So even though I know he can't come today—the necessary preliminaries haven't yet taken place—I know that he'll inspect what I've done today when he does come. Plenty of incentive there.

SIDEBAR

Armageddon as a Battle, Not a War

A reading of Revelation 16:12–16; 17:14; 19:11–21 shows that at least in this book of the Bible, the Battle of Armageddon is just that—a battle, not a war taking place over a more or less prolonged period in the last part of the tribulation (as taught by some pretribulationists). These texts indicate that the battle will take place right at Jesus' coming after the tribulation. Even if they didn't and the battle were really a war of some duration, its placement in the last part of the tribulation would make the associated coming of Jesus as a thief chronologically out of place for the pretrib argument that unexpectedness demands imminence, and imminence an occurrence before the tribulation.

Some teachers of pretribulationism recognize that despite a chapter break (which in any case wasn't introduced till many centuries after Paul wrote), the Day of the Lord in 1 Thessalonians 5:1–11 starts with his coming as described in 1 Thessalonians 4:13–18. Paul uses "Lord" for both the coming and the day. He speaks of both the Lord and the Day of the Lord as coming. And he makes the coming of the Day of the Lord an object of Christians' watching just as elsewhere he, in common with other writers of the New Testament and Jesus himself, makes the coming of the Lord an object of Christians' watching (see, for example, Phil. 3:20). The equation between the Lord's coming and the coming of the Day of the Lord could hardly be clearer.

The Unity of the Coming of the Day of the Lord with the Coming of the Lord Himself

Yet other teachers of pretribulationism recognize how severe a problem they then have in Paul's saying that the Day of the Lord can't come—which is the same as saying that the Lord himself can't come—till after the rebellion and revelation of the Antichrist. So they try to distinguish between the coming of the Lord in 1 Thessalonians 4:13–18 and the coming of the Day of the Lord in 1 Thessalonians 5:1–11. Their argument is that the phrase which opens chapter 5, "Now concerning," appears elsewhere in Paul's writings to introduce a new topic

"Now Concerning"

("Now concerning spiritual gifts" in 1 Cor. 12:1, for example, after a discussion of the Lord's Supper) and therefore the coming of the Day of the Lord, being introduced by this phrase, must differ from the coming of the Lord, just described.

A Shift but No Shift

In answer to this argument, the phrase "Now concerning" does introduce a new topic—true. But the new topic is the need of Christians to be watchful for the coming of the Day of the Lord. The earlier topic was the comfort they could get from the fact that their deceased fellow Christians would participate with them in the coming of the Lord. There's nothing here to make a *chronological* distinction between two comings, the Lord's at one time and that of the Day of the Lord at a later time, whether seven or more years later or just a short time later. By the same token, it's false to say that in posttribulationism the rapture at the Lord's coming precedes the coming of the Day of the Lord.

The Coming of the Day of the Lord as an Object of Watchfulness

Sometimes pretrib teachers will also deny that Paul makes the coming of the Day of the Lord an object of Christians' watchfulness. Again, it's true that in 1 Thessalonians 5:6 the exhortation, "Let us watch. . . ," has no object expressed in its own clause. Nor does the continuation, ". . . and stay sober." But watchfulness and sobriety in view of what? The coming of the Day of the Lord, with which the whole of the surrounding passage deals.

Grammatically speaking, the verb for being watchful, like the verb for staying sober, isn't the kind of verb that takes a direct object. You have to look at subject matter in the context to discover the object in view.

And here the coming of the Day of the Lord "as a thief" on the wicked but not in that way on Christians shows specifically what should be obvious in general, that watching has to do with the day and its coming.

In 2 Thessalonians 2:3, Paul recognizes that seeds of "the rebellion" are already germinating ("For the mystery of lawlessness is already at work"—verse 7). But he doesn't allow for the view that the rebellion reaches a climax before the rapture and that the man of lawlessness will be revealed when he makes a covenant with Israel at the start of Daniel's seventieth week, the tribulation (as in Dan. 9:27). The making of a covenant as mentioned by Daniel doesn't enter Paul's picture. He leaves it out. But he does describe in some detail the Antichrist's opposition to God, self-exaltation to the status of a deity who demands that others worship him, and so on (verses 4–12). And Paul says that this rebellion comes first, not that the rapture does (verse 3 again).

The Rebellion of the Antichrist as His Revelation

So the Pauline context disfavors a reference to covenant-making at the beginning of Daniel's seventieth week and favors instead a reference to the lawless man's pretensions to deity throughout the second half, from his breaking of the treaty at midweek onward. Such pretensions will certainly reveal his identity to alert and informed believers. Even if the making of a covenant were to have entered Paul's picture as the event which reveals the man of lawlessness for who he is, the coming of that revelation first—that is, before the Day of the Lord comes—would mean that Christians still couldn't watch for the Day of the Lord as imminent, as capable of happening at any moment. And since the making of a covenant will start the seventieth week, Christians would already have entered the tribulation.

Knowing and Not Knowing the Times and Seasons

Jesus' telling the disciples that it's not for them "to know the times or seasons which the Father has set by his own authority" (Acts 1:7) might seem to disagree with Paul's saying that the Thessalonian Christians don't need instruction on the times and seasons because he has already told them (1 Thess. 5:1; 2 Thess. 2:5). But Jesus is responding to a Jewish question whether he's going to restore the kingdom to Israel immediately (Acts 1:6), and he's saying in effect that the disciples should turn their attention to evangelizing all peoples throughout the world (Acts 1:8). Later, Paul will instruct the largely Gentile Christians in Thessalonica on the times and seasons leading up to the second coming (see again 2 Thess. 2:1–4 with 1 Thess. 5:1–5). Jesus has done the same, even earlier than his brushing aside the question of when he will restore the kingdom to Israel (see again especially Luke 21:28, 31, since Luke wrote the Gospel of Luke as well as the Acts of the Apostles [Acts 1:1 with Luke 1:1–4]).

The Relevance of Jesus' Teaching to the Church

Because Jesus is speaking to his Jewish disciples prior to the church age, some teachers of pretribulationism rule out his commands to watch for a second coming after the tribulation so far as Christians are concerned. Those commands don't apply to the church, they say; rather, only to those Jews and Gentiles who convert during the tribulation, after the rapture of Christians.

But wait a minute! The Jewish disciples to whom Jesus is speaking became the apostles of the Christian church, part of its very foundation (Eph. 2:20; compare Rev. 21:14). The Gospels in which his commands are recorded were written during the church age for Christians (see especially Matt. 16:17–19, "I will build my church," and 18:17, "tell the church"). In the Great Commission he tells these disciples to teach their converts, members of the Christian church, "to keep all things whatever I have commanded you." Surely these things include Jesus' commands to watch for the second coming "immediately after the tribulation" (Matt. 28:16–20 with 24:29). Paul makes "the words of our Lord Jesus Christ" a test of orthodoxy for the church (1 Tim. 6:3), uses those words in his own teaching to Christians (1 Cor. 7:10–11 with Matt. 5:31–32; 19:9; Mark 10:10–11; Luke 16:18 on divorce), and even borrows from Jesus the figure of coming "as a thief at night" (compare 1 Thess. 5:2, 4 with Matt. 24:42–44; Luke 12:39–40; also 2 Peter 3:10; Rev. 3:3; 16:15).

Cancellation of the seven thunders entails the cutting off of "those days" of tribulation, so that it's not enough for pretribulationism to say that the tribulation will run a full seven years and only the *plans* of the Antichrist will be cut short of fulfillment by God's bringing the tribulation to a close. Besides, the closest Jesus comes to talking about the Antichrist and his plans is "the abomination of desolation"—not much of a basis for interpreting the cutting off of those days as a cutting short of the Antichrist's plans.

Misplaced Efforts to Avoid a Shortening of the Trib

According to an alternative pretrib interpretation, the full seven years are already a shortened period. What, then, would the longer period have been? Doesn't the number "seven" indicate completeness, and a cutting short indicate *in*completeness, so that an incomplete period of seven years would produce an anomaly? The past tense of "has cut off" in Mark 13:20 doesn't support the view of seven years as an already shortened period, because the future tense of "will be cut off" in the parallel Matthew 24:22 shows Mark's past tense to be like a "prophetic perfect" in which a future action is portrayed as so certain to be done that we might as well speak of it as done.

Another alternative pretrib interpretation takes the cutting off as a reference to the suddenness and ferocity with which Jesus' return terminates the tribulation. But as shown by the purpose of preventing the destruction of all flesh, his statement has to do with length of time, not with manner of termination.

And yet another alternative pretrib interpretation says that the cutting off of those days means that individually the days of tribulation won't last twenty-four hours. Well, at least the hour, if not the day, of Christ's return still couldn't be calculated. At this point the argument gets silly. Is it really necessary to go through such contortions to evade the perfectly natural meaning that God won't allow the tribulation to run its full course, so that nobody can know the day or hour of Jesus' return though events of the tribulation which God does allow to occur will signal to Christian believers the general nearness of that return?

A Question of Nonfulfilment   Someone may object that a shortening of the tribulation would unacceptably entail the nonfulfilment of Daniel's prophecy concerning the length of the tribulation as seven full years. But the objection would carry a double-edge. For failure to shorten the tribulation would equally entail a nonfulfilment of Jesus' prophecy that the tribulation will be shortened.

It may also be objected that the nonfulfilments of Isaiah's prophecy concerning the time of King Hezekiah's death (2 Kings 20:1–11) and of Jonah's prophecy concerning the time of Nineveh's destruction (Jonah 3:1–10) are matters of historical record, not of interpretation. But this further objection wouldn't take into account that those past nonfulfilments establish the scriptural acceptability of nonfulfilments due to the mercy of God, as in the case before us. So there's no theological need to sacrifice the natural meaning of Jesus' prophecy that those days of tribulation will be cut off.

Despite all the evidence we've surveyed, suppose that Jesus' commands to watch were discounted. We'd still have Paul's commands to watch for an event that can't take place till after the rebellion and revelation of the Antichrist during the tribulation. And we'd still have Revelation 16:15, addressed to Christians in churches and talking about watching at the end of the tribulation for Jesus' coming as a thief. It's past time to give up the pretrib argument from watching. Some passages that mention watching don't discuss it in any detail, but those that do consistently direct our attention to Jesus' coming after the tribulation.

Posttrib Watching apart from Jesus' Teaching

SEIZING THE DAY   4

The popular Latin proverb, *Carpe diem* (pronounced KAR-peh DEE-em), means "Seize the day." In other words, take full advantage of present opportunities. Here I give it a different spin, so that it means to apprehend the Day of the Lord mentally, to understand it even more fully than in the preceding chapter.

Understanding the Day of the Lord

Just as Paul the Apostle writes that the Day of the Lord can't come unless the Antichrist's rebellion and revelation come first (2 Thess. 2:1–5), the prophet Joel says that "the sun will be turned into darkness and the moon into blood before the coming of the great and terrible Day of the LORD"[1] (Joel 2:30–31; compare verses 10–11: "The sun and moon grow dark, and the stars diminish in their brightness"; Isa. 13:6–10, especially verse 10: "For the stars of heaven . . . will not give their light, the sun will be darkened . . . , and the moon will not cause

Celestial Disasters that Follow the Trib but Precede the Day of the Lord

1. Here and below, the capital letters of "LORD" indicate a translation of the Hebrew divine title, "Yahweh" or "Jehovah."

its light to shine"; 34:4: "And the heavens will be rolled up like a scroll, and their host will fall down"; Ezek. 32:7: "I will cover the heavens and darken their stars; I will cover the sun with a cloud, and the moon will not give her light"). Yet Jesus, borrowing such language from the Old Testament, makes these celestial disasters follow the tribulation and introduce his return at that time:

> And immediately after the tribulation of those days, the sun will be darkened; and the moon will not give her light; and the stars will fall from heaven; and the powers of the heavens will be shaken; and then will appear the sign of the Son of man in heaven, and then all the tribes of the earth will mourn, and they will see the Son of man coming on the clouds of heaven with power and much glory (Matt. 24:29–31; similarly, Mark 13:24–26; Luke 21:25–27; compare Rev. 6:12–17).

Armageddon as Preceding the Day of the Lord

Seconding Jesus' placement of the celestial disasters right after the tribulation is Joel's placement of them at what is known from the New Testament as the Battle of Armageddon, when the posttribulational return of Christ takes place: "The sun and moon will grow dark and the stars will diminish their brightness" in connection with the LORD's judging the nations "in the valley of decision," or "Valley of Jehoshaphat," by treading the winepress, "for their wickedness is great" (Joel 3:9–16, excerpts; compare similar language, including the treading of a winepress, for the Battle of Armageddon in Rev. 14:17–20; 16:14–16; 19:11–16, this last passage including a detailed description of what everybody agrees is Jesus' return after the tribulation). First the tribulation, and then in quick succession the celestial disasters which are followed, again quickly, by the Day of the Lord, at which time he comes back. Confirmed: the Day of the Lord that Paul tells Christians to watch for (1 Thess. 5:1–10) doesn't begin till after the tribulation, so that Christians will stay on earth right through that period. Otherwise they wouldn't have to watch for it. They wouldn't *be able* to watch for it!

Elijah's Return as Preceding the Day of the Lord

Just as Joel puts celestial disasters before the coming of the Day of the LORD, so also another Old Testament prophet puts the sending back of Elijah before that day: "Behold, I ['the LORD of hosts'] will send you Elijah before the great and dreadful Day of the LORD" (Mal. 4:5). Since the time of the early church fathers, one of the two witnesses in Revelation 11:3–12 has regularly been identified with Elijah. Generally, pretribulationists agree to this identification—with good reason. Not only do we have Malachi's prophecy. We also have the statement of Jesus, "Elijah is indeed coming" (Matt. 17:11), and he made this statement after the martyrdom of John the Baptist. So even though "Elijah has already come" in the person of "John the Baptist" (verses 12–13), his predicted coming awaits a future fulfilment, too (compare Mark 9:11–13: "coming first, Elijah will restore all things").

Two Witnesses as Preceding the Day of the Lord

Who better to fulfil that prediction than one of the two witnesses in Revelation 11:3–12? No one, because those witnesses not only repeat the miracles of Moses by turning waters to blood and striking the earth "with every plague as many times as

they wish" (verse 6; compare Exod. 7:17,
19–20 and others of the ten plagues on
Egypt). They also repeat the miracles of Elijah by shutting up heaven, or the sky, so
that it doesn't rain, and by slaying their en-
emies with a fire that "consumes" them
(verses 5–6; compare 1 Kings 17:1: "Now
Elijah the Tishbite . . . said to Ahab, 'As the
LORD the God of Israel lives, before whom I
stand, there will be neither dew nor rain
these years, except at my word'" [a drought
follows]; James 5:17: "Elijah prayed ear-
nestly . . . that it might not rain, and for
three years and six months it did not rain
on the earth"; 2 Kings 1:10: "but Elijah an-
swered and spoke to the captain of fifty, 'If
I am a man of God, let fire come down from
heaven and consume you and your fifty.'
Then fire came down from heaven and consumed him and his fifty" [repeated almost
word for word in verse 12]).

For our purposes it doesn't matter
whether the two witnesses in Revelation
11:3–12 should be taken individually and
identified with Elijah and Moses, or
whether the two witnesses should be taken
collectively for all the saints on earth. If individually, they may be taken as personally
identical with the Old Testament figures of
those names (John the Baptist seems not to
have been personally identical with Elijah)
or as virtually identical because of playing
similar roles (compare the prophecy that
John the Baptist would come "in the spirit
and power of Elijah"—Luke 1:17). If collectively, Elijah and Moses provide a pattern
for the saints' activity; and the number
"two" symbolizes sufficiency of testimony,
since "every matter shall be established in

the mouth of two or three witnesses" (Deut. 19:15; Matt. 18:16; 2 Cor. 13:1; 1 Tim. 5:19).

What does matter to our question is the time during which the two witnesses testify. That is the second half of the tribulation, for "they will prophesy for 1,260 days," which equate with the "forty-two months" during which "the outer court of the temple . . . is given to the nations and they trample the holy city" (Rev. 11:2–3). This giving and trampling can hardly take place till the Antichrist breaks his covenant with Israel in the middle of the tribulation (Dan. 9:27— against viewing the two witnesses as martyred at the covenant-breaking in midweek, for that view impossibly requires the giving and trampling to take place while Antichrist is still honoring his covenant).

So there we have it: in one sense or another, Elijah will return before the Day of the Lord comes. In one sense or another, one of the two witnesses in Revelation 11:3–12 is the returned Elijah. His return occupies the second half of the tribulation. Since his return is said to precede the coming of the Day of the Lord, that day cannot include the tribulation. And since Paul tells Christians to watch for that day, they must expect to stay on earth throughout the tribulation.

To get around these straightforward arguments from Scripture, teachers of pretribulationism often but not always distinguish between the Day of the Lord and the Day of Christ, and say that the church's rapture will occur at the Day of Christ before the tribulation, the Day of the Lord following at a later date. But this distinction wouldn't work even if it could be made legitimately. It wouldn't work because what-

The Day of the Lord as Equivalent to the Day of Christ

ever the Day of Christ means, Paul told Christians to watch for the Day of the Lord.

And the distinction is false in the first place. Paul uses "Lord" exclusively or almost exclusively for Christ, so that, for example, "God" stands for the Father, "Lord" for Christ the Son, and "Spirit" for the third person of the Trinity in passages such as 1 Corinthians 12:4–6; 2 Corinthians 13:13; Ephesians 1:3 (with the adjective form of "Spirit," but still in reference to the Holy Spirit—compare verse 13); 4:4–6. The very common addition of "Jesus Christ" to "Lord" shows that for Paul "Lord" and "Christ" point to the same person. So also does the placement of "Christ Jesus" ahead of "Lord." "You serve the Lord Christ" (Col. 3:24) proves the same point.

Furthermore, to distinguish the Day of Christ from the Day of the Lord overlooks the fact that Paul uses a much wider variety of expressions than these two. "Day of Christ" appears in Philippians 1:10; 2:16, and "Day of the Lord" in 1 Corinthians 5:5 (according to the best manuscripts); 1 Thessalonians 5:2; 2 Thessalonians 2:2. But "Day of Christ Jesus" appears in Philippians 1:6 (where some inferior manuscripts have "Day of Jesus Christ"), "Day of our Lord Jesus" in 2 Corinthians 1:14, and "Day of our Lord Jesus Christ" in 1 Corinthians 1:8. If you're going to make the Day of the Lord and the Day of Christ refer to different events, why not make the Day of Christ and the Day of the Lord Jesus refer to different events? In wording, "Day of the Lord Jesus" is just as different from "Day of Christ" as "Day of the Lord" is. And so on with regard to all the variations. It makes no more sense to refer the various expressions to different events than it does to refer "Jesus," "Christ," "Lord," "Lord Jesus," "Lord Christ," and "Lord Jesus Christ" to different persons. To top it off, none of the variations on "Day of the Lord" occur in passages that provide any argument for pretribulationism.

More on the Two Witnesses as Elijah and Moses

Fire comes "out of the mouth" of the two witnesses in Revelation 11:5, but "from heaven" in 2 Kings 1:10, 12. This difference shouldn't trouble us, though, because "out of the mouth" doesn't have to do with fire-breathing but means simply that lightning strikes from the sky in response to spoken words, such as Elijah's.

Some would substitute Enoch for Moses, because like Elijah, but unlike Moses, Enoch never died. Yet the two witnesses' miracles favor Moses and Elijah over Enoch and Elijah. So, too, do the pairings of Moses and Elijah in accounts of the transfiguration (Matt. 17:1–9; Mark 9:2–10; Luke 9:28–36).

Nonfulfilment in John the Baptist

The return of Elijah in the person of John the Baptist has been used to argue that even though Elijah will return again during the tribulation, his past return satisfies Malachi's prophecy that Elijah will return before the Day of the Lord and thus allows that day to include the tribulation. This argument is followed up with the further argument that since at his future coming Elijah "will restore all things" (Matt. 17:11), the reference must be to Jesus' taking the role of Elijah at the second coming, not to a taking of that role by one of the two witnesses, for they suffer martyrdom rather than restoring everything (Rev. 11:7–13).

But it could be argued equally well that John the Baptist didn't satisfy Malachi's prophecy, because it says that at his return Elijah "will turn the hearts of fathers to their children and the hearts of children to their fathers," with the result that the LORD "will not come and strike the land with a curse [alternatively, 'with a ban of destruction']." Most of the Jewish people rejected John as well as Jesus, however (Matt. 11:18–19; 17:12–13; Mark 9:12b–13; Luke 7:33–35). John suffered martyrdom, too. And the Jews' land quickly fell under the curse of Roman destruction, including the destruction of Jerusalem and the temple in A.D. 70.

Despite the martyrdom of the two witnesses, on the other hand, their testimony bears the fruit of innumerable conversions (Rev. 7:9–17), and their resurrection and the turning of "the kingdom of the world" into "the kingdom of our Lord and of his Christ" follow quickly. Sounds much more like the restoration of all things than does the outcome of John the Baptist's ministry, doesn't it? And Jesus' distinguishing himself as the Son of man from Elijah (Matt. 17:11–12) goes against his taking Elijah's role at the second coming.

Distinguishing the Lord's Day from the Day of the Lord

A few teachers of pretribulationism interpret "the Lord's Day" in Revelation 1:10 as equivalent to the Day of the Lord. Then they argue that since John the seer received visions concerning the tribulation while he was "in the Spirit" on that day, it must include the tribulation. Apart from the resulting contradiction of several other passages that we've seen to put the Day of the Lord later than the tribulation, "Lord's" differs from "of the Lord" in the original Greek as well as in English. "Day of the Lord" is so stereotyped—it occurs many times in the Old Testament as well as in the New Testament—that John isn't likely to have changed "of the Lord" to "Lord's" if he had meant the same as "Day of the Lord." About the same time as he wrote the Book of Revelation, or shortly afterwards, other early Christian writers were using "Lord's Day" for the first day of the week, "Sunday" (Ignatius' *Epistle to the Magnesians* 9:1; *The Teaching of the Twelve Apostles* 14:1 [where the addition "of the Lord" to "Lord's Day" demonstrates the difference between "Lord's" and "of the Lord"]). Paul uses "Lord's" once elsewhere, with "Supper" (1 Cor. 11:20). It's attractive to think that Communion was called the Lord's Supper because it was ordinarily celebrated every Sunday, the Lord's Day, or that Sunday was called the Lord's Day because the Lord's Supper was ordinarily celebrated on it.

Similar attempts to make the Day of the Lord cover the tribulation rest on Old Testament passages that use the expression (Joel 2:1–2). But some of the passages cited to support this view don't use "the Day of the LORD" (Isa. 66:15–16), or they use "that day" without specifying that it's the Day of the LORD (Jer. 30:7). Others that do specify the Day of the LORD don't need to refer to the tribulation; they may refer to the immediately following Battle of Armageddon, for example, or to the LORD's doings in past history (Joel 2:32–3:21; Amos 5:18–20; Obad. 15–16; Zeph. 2:1–5; Zech. 14:1–21).

Distinguishing the Day of the Lord from the Tribulation

A No Good Gap

Some teachers of pretribulationism have not only made the Day of the Lord cover the tribulation but have also posited a gap, probably short, between a prior rapture of the church and the start of that day, so that the rapture doesn't lead immediately into the tribulation but precedes it by a space of time. The purpose of this hypothesis is to make the entirety of the tribulation a time of God's wrath yet keep Christians at least a little apart from that day of wrath even at its inception. But even if short, such a gap makes nonsense of Paul's telling Christians to watch for the coming of the Day of the Lord.

The Falsehood of Peace and Safety

Yet again, a few have argued that since the Day of the Lord arrives at a time of peace and safety (1 Thess. 5:2–3), it will have to arrive before the tribulation, for the tribulation will shatter all peace and safety. Here we have another oversight. Paul doesn't say that there will *be* peace and safety at the time the Day of the Lord arrives. Rather, non-Christians will be *"saying,* 'Peace and safety.'" You can't help but think of the similar Old Testament passages, Jeremiah 6:14 and 8:11: "They have healed the wound of my people superficially, saying, 'Peace, peace,' when there is no peace" (see also Ezek. 13:10). Maybe Paul had those passages in mind. In any case, the contrast doesn't lie between peace–safety and sudden destruction as such, but between the saying of peace and safety and the coming of sudden destruction. We might also compare the three days' merriment of the wicked at the end of the tribulation, when the Beast kills the Lord's two witnesses (Rev. 11:7–10).

Not Destined for God's Wrath 5

A Promise of Exemption

The same passage that tells Christians to be watchful for the Day of the Lord also assures them that God hasn't destined them for his wrath, but to obtain salvation through their Lord Jesus Christ (1 Thess. 5:9; see also John 3:36; 5:24; Rom. 5:9; 8:1; Eph. 2:3; 5:6; 1 Thess. 1:10). And since God will pour out his wrath on earth during the tribulation—as already noted, the plagues in the seven bowls of Revelation 15:1, 7; 16:1–21 are explicitly called "the wrath of God"—somehow Christians have to be gone despite Paul's telling them that the Day of the Lord for which they're to watch won't come unless the rebellion and revelation of the Antichrist come first. So goes the next thought that pops into your mind if you've been taught a pretrib rapture.

But think again. The Book of Revelation puts saved people in the tribulation. Lots of them, in fact:

The Undeniable Presence of Saved People in the Tribulation

> After these things I looked, and behold, a great crowd whom no one could number,

47

from every nation and all tribes and peoples and tongues, standing before the throne and before the Lamb, clothed with white robes and palm branches in their hands. And they shout with a loud voice, saying, "Salvation to our God who sits on the throne, and to the Lamb." . . . And one of the elders asked me, saying, "Who are these people clothed with white robes, and where did they come from?" And I said to him, "Sir, you know." And he told me, "These are the ones coming out of the great tribulation, and they have washed their robes and whitened them by the blood of the Lamb. And on account of this they are before the throne of God, and they serve him day and night in his temple. And the one sitting on the throne will shelter them. They will not hunger any more. Neither will they thirst any more. Neither will the sun or any scorching heat fall on them, because the Lamb in the midst of the throne will shepherd them and lead them to springs of the water of life. And God will wipe away every tear from their eyes" (Rev. 7:9–10, 11–17).

Now if there ever was a description of salvation from God's wrath, that's it. Yet the people who enjoy this salvation will live on earth during the tribulation, as nobody disputes. Because that's what the text says: "These are the ones coming out of the great tribulation" (verse 14).

The Undeniable Presence of Saints in the Tribulation   Elsewhere the Book of Revelation calls these people "saints" (see especially 13:7, which reports that the Beast will make war against the saints and conquer them, that is, persecute them to the point of martyrdom; also 5:8; 8:3, 4; 11:18; 13:10; 14:12; 16:6; 17:6; 18:20, 24; 19:8). The Book of

Revelation also describes them as those "who die in the Lord," which—since Christ is Lord—sounds remarkably like "the dead in Christ" who Paul says will participate in the rapture of the church (1 Thess. 4:16–18; compare 1 Cor. 15:18), and describes them yet further as those "who keep the commandments of God and have the testimony of Jesus" (Rev. 12:17; see very similar descriptions in 6:9; 14:12; 19:10; 20:4 with 1:9, where John, himself a Christian and apostle of the church, writes as an exile on the Island of Patmos "because of the word of God and the testimony of Jesus").

There can be no doubt, then, that saved people will live on earth during the tribulation. Informed pretribulationists freely admit as much. Only they don't regard these people as belonging to the church, since in their view the church left before the tribulation began. Now here's the rub if you want to argue that the salvation of Christians from God's wrath requires their absence during the tribulation. Take those saints who come out of that period. What kind of salvation are they celebrating if not a salvation from God's wrath? Washed white in the blood of the Lamb yet suffering the wrath of God because they missed a pretrib rapture? Is that what we're supposed to think about them? Of course not. Well, then, neither can you argue that the salvation of Christians from God's wrath will require *their* absence during the tribulation.

The Nonequation of Exemption with Absence

But what is tribulation anyway? The term refers to distresses of various sorts, including persecution, and attains prominence in connection with an endtime pe-

The Church as Always Enduring Tribulation

riod of unprecedentedly severe and widespread distresses known as *the* tribulation (Matt. 24:9, 21, 29; Mark 13:19, 24; Rev. 7:14). Christians have never been promised exemption from tribulation in general. On the contrary, they've been told they will suffer it (John 16:33; Acts 14:22; Rom. 5:3; 1 Thess. 3:3; Rev. 1:9; 2:10). And they *have* suffered it, sometimes less, sometimes more, sometimes with great bloodshed. So there's nothing about the tribulation as such that requires the church's absence. Quite the reverse!

The Church as Always Encountering Antichrists

Similarly, the fact that the church has confronted lesser antichrists throughout her history favors the church's confrontation with *the* Antichrist at the end of history, during the tribulation ("just as you have heard that Antichrist is coming, even now many antichrists have come on the scene"—1 John 2:18, 22; 4:3). So what if persecution by the Antichrist will exceed any previous persecution? In the nature of the case, one persecution is liable to exceed all others, but that fact offers no reason to exempt the church from the worst persecution and put that persecution onto later saints, the delay in whose conversion would in many cases be due to the church's failure to evangelize them before the tribulation. Some justice!

A House of Horrors

Persecution doesn't exhaust the horrors of the tribulation, though. Other horrors stemming from human wickedness include the succession of militarism, warfare, famine, and death, one growing out of the other (Rev. 6:1–8). Yet other horrors will stem from Satanic and demonic activity, such as widespread demon possession, which will be limited, however, to those "who do not have God's seal on their foreheads" (Rev. 9:1–11). The plagues of the fifth and sixth trumpets, which equate with the first and second woes, are likewise limited to "the earth-dwellers," a term used in the Book of Revelation to distinguish unbelievers from the saints (8:13–9:21).

Directly or indirectly, of course, Christians have always suffered from the horrors perpetrated by wicked people and fomented by Satan and his demons. So from that standpoint there's no reason to suppose tribulational horrors of those sorts will require the church's absence. As in the case of persecution, unprecedented intensity and range make no difference, for we know and agree that saved people of one kind or another will be on earth during the tribulation.

Back to God's wrath, then. No saved person can suffer it—that much is clear. So whoever they are, saints of the tribulation won't have the bowls of God's wrath poured out on them. In fact, there are indications right within the description of those bowls that the wrath in them will fall only on unbelievers.

The Limitation of God's Wrath to Unbelievers

It's said explicitly that the first bowl will be directed against those who "have the mark of the Beast and worship his image" (Rev. 16:2; see also 14:9–10) and the second and third against those who "shed the blood of saints and prophets" (16:6). The fourth and fifth against those who in response "blasphemed the name of God . . . and did not repent so as to give him glory" (16:9), and "blasphemed the God of heaven . . . and did not repent of their deeds" (16:11). The sixth bowl has to do with those who gather to fight against God Almighty at Armageddon (16:12–16; see also 14:19; 19:15), and the seventh with the fall of Babylon, out of which God's people have been called "in order not to receive her plagues" (16:17–21; 18:3–4; see also 14:8). The objects of the seventh respond again with blasphemy (16:21). All these scriptural data make it as clear as day that whatever other horrors saints will suffer during the tribulation, as they have often suffered throughout history, those horrors will not include the wrath of God contained in the bowls. That wrath will fall only on the ungodly.

The Limitation of God's Wrath to the End of the Trib

But when? Over the whole period of tribulation, or at least its second half? Not likely. Revelation 15:1 calls the plagues of the seven bowls containing God's wrath "the last." Coming as it does after the descriptions of plagues under the seven seals and in the seven trumpets, and after cancellation of the seven thunders, this description naturally indicates that God will concentrate his wrath at the very close of the tribulation, not spread it out over the whole or second half. It's easier to understand, then, how saints can stay on earth during the tribulation without suffering that wrath.

The Combination of Presence with Exemption

Earlier passages in the Book of Revelation prove the possibility—indeed, the actuality—of presence in the tribulation combined with exemption from God's wrath. Chapter 6 closes with the question, "For the great day of their wrath [God's and the Lamb's] has come, and who is able to stand?" (verse 17). Chapter 7 opens with a command to four angels that they hold back the winds, that is, winds of wrath, till the servants of God have been sealed for exemption (verses 1–3). Chapter 7 then closes with a vision of the innumerable company of redeemed people who have come out of the tribulation (verses 9–17). Their posture: "standing" (verse 9).

Here we have John's answer to the question of who can't be blown down or away, but can stand, when God vents the winds of his wrath against the world. It's the redeemed, those whose robes are washed white by the blood of the Lamb and whose foreheads are marked with God's seal. *They* will stand, for just as having "the mark of the Beast" exposes its bearers to God's wrath though exempting them from that of the Beast, so having "the seal of the living God" exempts its bearers from his wrath though exposing them to the wrath of the Beast (13:16–17; 14:9–11; 16:2; 19:20; 20:4).

Kept from the Hour as Exemption from Its Testing

Even earlier in the Book of Revelation there appears a promise of exemption for true Christians: "Because you have kept my word of patience, I [Jesus] also will keep you from the hour of testing that is going to come on the whole inhabited earth to test the ones dwelling on the earth" (3:10). As noted before and generally agreed, these earth-dwellers do *not* include the saints. They can't, because elsewhere they appear as killers of the martyrs (6:10) and objects of the three last woes (8:13). They gloat over the murder of God's two witnesses for those witnesses' having tormented them (11:10), and they get drunk with the wine of fornication of the harlot Babylon (17:2). All of them worship the Beast, and none of them have their names written in the Lamb's book of life (13:8, 12, 14; 17:8). These statements concerning the earth-dwellers exclude from their number the saints who live alongside them during "the hour of testing." So whatever other sufferings these saints have to endure during the tribulation, the hour of testing that will come on the earth-dwellers is not among them.

Kept from the Hour as Opposed to Being Taken out of the World

Why not? Because Jesus will keep them from that hour. Now pretribulational teachers usually appeal to this promise as though it means that Jesus will take Christians out of the world ahead of time so that they won't even be here during the hour of testing. But in the only other New Testament passage where according to the original Greek the phrase "keep from" appears—that is, in John 17:15, spoken by Jesus and reported by John just as in Revelation 3:10, so that you'd expect a similar usage—in that passage "keep from" is put in opposition to "take out of the world." Here it is, a prayer of Jesus for his disciples: "I do not ask that you would take them out of the world, but that you would keep them from the Evil One [that is, Satan]."

Are we then to believe that Jesus' keeping Christians from the hour of testing equates with taking them out of the world, or at least results from taking them out of it? No, just as Christians are kept from Satan while they're in the world, where he's a threat, so they'll be kept from the hour of testing while they're on earth, where that hour is a threat (see also John 17:11, 12; 1 John 5:18 for keeping in the sense of protection while in the world, as opposed to removal from the world). What looked like a prooftext for pretribulationism turns out to favor the church's presence on earth during the tribulation.

And especially during the last part of it—in other words, right through to the end. For although "the hour of testing" is usually taken to mean the whole tribulation, or at least the last three and a half years of it, "hour" carries a much narrower meaning elsewhere in the Book of Revelation. At 3:3 it refers to the hour of Jesus' return. At 9:13–19, to what looks like the Battle of Armageddon, connected with Jesus' return (compare 16:12–16). At 11:13, to the great earthquake that occurs at the end of the tribulation's second half (see verses 1–3) and shakes "the great city" (compare verse 8 and the fall of Babylon in 14:8 and chapters 17–18; also 6:12; 8:5; 11:19; 16:18 for the final earthquake). At 14:7–8; 17:12; 18:10, 17, 19, "hour" refers explicitly to the fall of Babylon at the close of the tribulation, and at 17:12 also to the related Battle of Armageddon. Finally, at 14:15 "hour" refers to a reaping of "the harvest of the earth" that is "fully ripe"— and the reaper is "one like a son of man sitting on the cloud [and] having on his head a gold crown," a description harking back to that of Jesus and his return (1:7 ["Behold, he is coming with the clouds"], 13 ["girded around the chest with a gold belt"]; compare Dan. 7:13; Matt. 24:30; 26:64; Mark 13:26; 14:62; Luke 21:27; Acts 1:11; 1 Thess. 4:16–17).

So elsewhere in the Book of Revelation, "hour" connects only with the final crisis of the tribulation, at which God pours out his

The Hour of Testing as Final Crisis, Not the Whole Trib

wrath on the wicked and at the conclusion of which Jesus comes back. Therefore "the hour of testing" from which he will keep Christians would seem to connect with that same crisis and not refer to a period of tribulation prolonged over seven or three and a half years. And since, as we have seen, "keep from" means exemption by protection on earth rather than exemption by removal from the world, once again what looked like a prooftext for pretribulationism turns out to favor Christians' staying here throughout, being protected from God's wrath in the final crisis of the tribulation, and then being raptured at Jesus' return just afterward.

Escaping as Emergence, Not Nonentry

Luke 21:36 requires much less comment. There Jesus tells his disciples to pray that they might be able "to escape all these things that are going to happen" (the events of the tribulation) and consequently "to stand before the Son of man" (whose return has just been described). In the first place, the context has spoken only about the Son of man's coming *after* the tribulation (verses 25–27). In the second place, Luke uses the verb "escape" elsewhere only in Acts 16:27; 19:16, and neither time does it mean avoidance of entrance—rather, exit from within (escaping out of a jail in the first instance, out of a house in the second). So escaping the events of the tribulation hardly means nonentrance into it; rather, coming out of it with your faith intact so as to enjoy the presence of the returned Christ. Yet again, what looked like proof of a pretrib rapture turns out to favor the church's presence on earth during the tribulation. Not destined for God's wrath: true. Not destined for staying here: false.

Nonminutiae

Though "hour" probably refers to the final crisis of the tribulation, it doesn't need to mean an hour of sixty minutes. The ancient Greek language in which the New Testament was originally written didn't even have a word for minutes. Nor does modern usage require an hour of sixty minutes. Webster gives "a short indefinite period of time" as another possible meaning.

Protection and Obedience

"Keep" can have other meanings besides "protect," as in "keeping" commandments by way of obeying them. Even there, however, the obedience protects them by keeping them from being broken, that is, disobeyed. And the meaning of protection is guaranteed and highlighted in Revelation 3:10 by the closely attached element of "testing," just as in John 17:15 the closely attached element of "the Evil One" dictates that "keep" means "protect" there, too.

Earth-Dwellers

"The whole inhabited earth" on which the hour of testing comes doesn't imply that all the earth's inhabitants will be tested by the hour, only that "the earth-dwellers" are to be found throughout habitable parts of the earth. As before, the earth-dwellers are to be distinguished from the saints, who though living on earth do not belong to it (compare Jesus' disciples' being *in* the world but not *of* it—John 17:6, 11, 14, 16).

Time as Experienced, Not as Such

The argument that being kept from a person ("the Evil One") makes John 17:15 fundamentally different from Revelation 3:10, which talks about a period of time ("the hour of testing"), doesn't fly. In the first place, it doesn't disturb the use of "keep from" in opposition to the action of removal. Then also, it's obvious that the promise in Revelation 3:10 doesn't have to do with a time period *as such* any more than Jesus' "hour" in John's Gospel refers to a period of time *as such* rather than to a period of time *as experienced*—in Jesus' case, experienced as crucifixion; in the earth-dwellers' case, experienced as testing (compare John 2:4; 7:30; 8:20; 12:23, 27; 13:1; 17:1). The really operative part of the expression "the hour of testing" is the phrase "of testing." If not, there wouldn't be any need for protection.

Jeremiah 30:7 speaks about the Jews' being saved from the time of Jacob's trouble. But even pretrib teachers don't understand that verse to mean salvation from a time as such; rather, from the trouble that characterizes this time. Similarly, being kept from the hour of testing doesn't mean protection from an hour as such; rather, from the testing that characterizes this hour. The hour hasn't yet started, of course, whereas Jeremiah portrays the time of Jacob's trouble as already in progress; and there's a difference between being *saved* from something already in progress and being *kept* from something that's yet to start. But the spatial and chronological point remains that if salvation from a time of trouble doesn't necessitate prior removal from the earth, neither does protection from an hour of testing necessitate prior removal from the earth.

There are further differences between Revelation 3:10 and John 17:15, of course. They don't affect the argument, however. Jesus' disciples were already in the world. The church isn't already in the hour of testing. But the parallel isn't between being kept from *the world* and being kept from the hour of testing. Rather, between being kept from *the Evil One* (because the disciples' being in the world creates a need for protection from him) and being kept from the hour of testing (because the church's being on earth creates a need for protection from the hour of testing). In both cases the protection is future. And just as protection from the Evil One doesn't come by way of physical removal from the world, where he pursues his nefarious activities, protection from the hour of testing doesn't come by way of physical removal from the earth, where the hour of testing takes effect.

Protection as Required by Presence

Some teachers of pretribulationism try to salvage Revelation 3:10 for their view by saying that the church will be kept outside the hour of testing just as according to John 17:15 Jesus prays that his disciples be kept outside the Evil One. But this explanation doesn't help pretribulationism. For if protection outside the Evil One is given the disciples while they're still in the world, it's only natural that protection outside the hour of testing will be given the church while she's still on earth. Just as it is presence in the world that creates a need for protection from the Evil One, so it is presence on earth that will create a need for protection from the hour of testing.

Presence as Requiring Protection

Yet other teachers of pretribulationism have taken to interpreting Revelation 3:10

by Joshua 2:13; Psalms 33:19; 56:13; Proverbs 21:23; Acts 15:29; and James 5:20. In all these latter passages, they argue, the preposition translated "from" indicates a position outside its object without implying an earlier position inside. Well and good, but this usage presents no argument against the posttrib meaning of Revelation 3:10. So long as it's recognized that "the hour of testing" comes only on the wicked, "the earth-dwellers"—which is exactly what the text says—the saints of the tribulation will be in a position outside that hour even though, as in pretribulationism, too, they are living here at the same time. Besides, the already-discussed parallel with John 17:15 is much closer than the parallels in the passages mentioned at the beginning of this paragraph.

The Protection of Israel

Several of the tribulational plagues—grievous sores, the turning of water to blood, thick darkness—match plagues that God sent on Egypt just before the exodus. God's protection of the Israelites from those plagues suggests the protection of saints from his wrath poured out at the end of the tribulation. So also does the repeated comparison in Revelation between the redemption of Israel at the exodus and the redemption of New Testament saints at Jesus' return following the tribulation (see, for example, 15:2–5). It's true, of course, that the Israelites were protected in a part of Egypt called Goshen, whereas Christians live throughout the world. But God left the Israelites where they were, as he would not do with the church if pretribulational teaching were true.

Similarly, Noah was protected on earth right through the Flood. (Enoch's translation occurred hundreds and hundreds of years before the Flood, and so doesn't have anything to do with the Flood or support a rapture of the church just or shortly before the tribulation.) Lot left Sodom before the fire and brimstone fell, but he didn't leave the plain. He stayed in another one of its cities and received protection there (Gen. 19:15–23). Rahab was still residing in Jericho when God felled its walls, and he saw to her protection (Josh. 6:17, 22–25). Ironically, these Old Testament episodes are often cited for a pretrib rapture when in fact they stand opposed to it.

The Protection of Noah, Lot, and Rahab

One teacher of pretribulationism has observed that even today, Christians feel the effects of God's wrath directed against the unsaved, and has drawn the conclusion that if God allowed Christians to enter the tribulation, they would feel the effects of his wrath then, too.[1] Does feeling the effects differ from feeling the wrath itself? Whether or not it does, this teacher seems to have forgotten that by making Christians feel those effects now, he has opened the way for Christians to feel those effects in the tribulation.

Feeling the Effects of God's Wrath

All teachers of pretribulationism ask how God could possibly protect Christians if he left them on earth during the tribulation, and fulminate that the distresses of the tribulation will be so severe and widespread that Christians will have to be removed beforehand if they're to be protected

The Possibility of Protection on Earth as Proved by the 144,000

---

1. Charles C. Ryrie, *Come Quickly, Lord Jesus* (Eugene, Oreg.: Harvest House, 1996) 109, 122.

at all. But these same pretrib teachers tell us that the 144,000 of Revelation 7:1–8; 14:1–5 are sealed for protection in order that they may evangelize the whole earth throughout the tribulation. What has happened to the impossibility of earthly protection? Let the teachers answer their own question!

Protection according to Jesus

Along the same line, Jesus' statement that no flesh would be saved unless the days of the tribulation were cut off "on account of the elect" (Matt. 24:22; Mark 13:20) has been used to argue that the disasters of that period will fall on saved and unsaved indiscriminately. But the clear statements of discrimination in the Book of Revelation flatly contradict this argument, and Jesus' statement itself may imply only that if those days weren't going to be cut off, the tribulation would become so severe as to make discrimination impossible. In the immediately preceding context, moreover, Jesus' commanding the disciples in Judea to flee into the mountains and to pray that they not have to take their flight in winter implies the possibility of protection for the elect up to whatever point at which those days are cut off (Matt. 24:15–21; Mark 13:14–19).

Late Wrath, Not Early Wrath

Some might think—do think, in fact—that John's not only describing the plagues poured out of seven bowls as "last," but also writing that in them the wrath of God is "finished" (Rev. 15:1), implies a pouring out of his wrath earlier in the tribulation. Also, since that wrath is about to strike already under the sixth seal (Rev. 6:12–17, especially verses 16–17) and does strike under the seventh seal (8:1–5, especially verse 5), it can't be true that God will concentrate his wrath at the end of the tribulation. The wrath must start early in the tribulation.

Though we were to draw such a conclusion, it would remain true that saved people can't suffer God's wrath no matter who they are or when he pours out his wrath. And it would remain true that saved people will be present on earth throughout the tribulation. But the pretrib conclusion doesn't follow, for there's plenty of evidence to support an understanding that the seventh in *each* series of plagues has to do with the end, when Christ comes back. First, consider the close similarity, often identity, of contents. The seventh seal contains half an hour of heavenly silence, the throwing of fire on the earth in answer to the prayers of persecuted saints (compare 6:9–11), peals of thunder, rumblings, flashes of lightning, and an earthquake (8:1–5). The seventh trumpet contains a statement that the kingdom of the world has become the kingdom of the Lord and of his Christ, a thanksgiving to the Lord God Almighty for his having taken control and begun to reign, for his exercising wrath, judging the dead, rewarding his servants, prophets, and saints, and for his destroying those who destroy the earth. The seventh trumpet also contains the opening of God's temple in heaven, a display of the ark of the covenant, flashes of lightning, rumblings, peals of thunder, an earthquake, and huge hailstones (11:15–19). And the seventh bowl contains the shout, "It has happened!" followed by the usual flashes of lightning, rumblings, peals of thunder, and an earthquake, plus the fleeing away of every island and mountain

The Finality of the Seventh Seal, Seventh Trumpet, and Seventh Bowl

and, once more, huge hailstones (16:17–
21). These parallels are so extensive as to
favor a common reference to the end, so
that each succeeding series of plagues steps
back and again works up to the end.

Second, consider the character of the
contents in each seventh. It is such as to
mark the end: a primeval-like silence broken by announcements of the judgment
and reward that have ushered in the new
age of God's kingdom on earth, an earthquake that causes the downfall of Babylon
in answer to the prayers of the saints persecuted by that harlot, and a revelation of the
heavenly Holy of holies. These are not re-
peatable events, nor are they suitably inter-
mediate. All of them refer to the end, when
Christ returns after the tribulation. So it remains likely that the wrath announced
under the sixth seal and inflicted under the
seventh is one and the same as the wrath
poured out of the seven bowls, "which are
the last" (15:1).

In confirmation, the souls of martyrs
under the heavenly altar in the fifth seal cry
out, "How long, Holy and True Sovereign,
will you not judge and exact vengeance for
our blood from the earth-dwellers?" (Rev.
6:10). So God's wrath hasn't yet struck. And
the stars' falling and the sun's becoming
black and the moon like blood under the
sixth seal (6:12–13) correspond to the stars'
falling, the sun's turning dark, and the
moon's not giving her light "immediately
after the tribulation" and just before the
coming of Jesus "with power and great
glory" (Matt. 24:29–30) to judge "all the nations" (Matt. 25:31).

As for "last" and "finished," they don't necessarily imply an earlier infliction of God's wrath. Even if they did, who's to say that he inflicted it during an earlier part of the tribulation rather than on occasions prior to the tribulation? All that "last" has to mean is that the plagues are poured out at the end, and all that "finished" has to mean is that the amount of wrath poured out is complete for the occasion in view. For everybody must agree that the drinking of God's wrath "forever and ever" in Revelation 14:10–11 represents a further occasion that limits the reference of "finished" in 15:1 to an earlier occasion at the end of the tribulation.

Last as Late, Finished as Complete

LEFT OUT   6

Pretribulationists warn that if people don't repent and believe in Christ now, they'll be left behind at the rapture and therefore have to suffer the horrors of the tribulation. In fact, a videotape with the title "Left Behind" has received nationwide distribution, and a novel of the same title has become a best-seller among religious books. Certainly people should be induced to exercise repentance and Christian faith, but with truth. What should occupy seekers of the truth about Jesus' return is what's left *out*, not who's left *behind*.

Left Out versus Left Behind, What versus Who

What's left out are explicit statements in the New Testament that Jesus will return before the tribulation. All the books of the New Testament were written in the age of the church by and for Christians who made up the church of the first century. Collectively, then, the New Testament is a preeminently Christian book. Now if Jesus really was going to come back before the tribulation for the purpose of taking Christians out of the world, you'd sure expect the New Testament to say so. After all, a pretrib rap-

What to Expect from the New Testament

ture would affect all Christians more directly and immediately than any other event of biblical prophecy would do. It would be designed solely for them.

Pretrib Failure of Expectation

Strikingly, though, the New Testament contains not even a single statement that says, "And immediately *before* the tribulation of those days, the Lord himself will descend from heaven; the dead in Christ will rise first; then we who are alive and remain will be caught up together with them to meet the Lord in the air," or words to that effect. Not in the Gospels. Not in the Acts of the Apostles. Not in the Epistles. Not in the Book of Revelation. Absolutely nowhere in the New Testament do we read such a statement or anything resembling it.

Posttrib Fulfilment of Expectation

What we do read are these statements: "And immediately *after* the tribulation of those days . . . they will see the Son of man coming on the clouds of heaven with power and great glory, and he will send his angels with a great trumpet and they will gather his elect . . ." (Matt. 24:29–31). "And in those days, *after* that tribulation . . . then people will see the Son of man coming in clouds with great power and glory, and then he will send the angels and they will gather his elect . . ." (Mark 13:24–27). Luke 21:25–28 speaks similarly.

Posttrib Redemption and Relief

Romans 8:18–23 puts one element of the rapture—"the redemption of our bodies" (that is, the resurrection of deceased Christians and the translation of living ones)—in conjunction with the liberation of the inanimate creation from "its bondage to decay," a bondage that attains its worst in the ecological plagues of the tribulation (compare Rev. 6:12–14; 7:1; 8:1–12; 11:6; 16:3–4, 8–9,

18–21). And 2 Thessalonians 1:5–10 puts the "relief" of Christians from their persecutions, not at a coming of Jesus before the tribulation to steal away the church and leave non-Christians behind to suffer the exponentially worsening terrors of the tribulation, but "at the revelation of the Lord Jesus from heaven with his mighty angels, in flaming fire rendering vengeance on those who do not know God and do not obey the gospel of our Lord Jesus."

By all accounts, as pretribulationists agree, those words describe the coming of Christ after the tribulation, not a coming beforehand. And it is there, not at an earlier coming, that Paul locates the cessation of persecution for the church as well as the punishment of the church's persecutors— despite a denial of the plain wording of Paul's text by a prominent pretribulationist: "The subject . . . is not release but *vindication*. . . . Second Thessalonians 1 does not teach that release from persecution will necessarily occur at the same time as the second coming. It does not picture the rapture at all."[1] Vindication—yes; but release by rapture, too. What else does Paul mean by writing that "it is right for God to give you, the ones being afflicted,[2] relief with us at the revelation of the Lord Jesus from heaven" and then adding "the coming of our Lord Jesus Christ and our being gath-

1. Ryrie, *Come Quickly, Lord Jesus,* pp. 59, 62.

2. Earlier in this same sentence, Paul referred to "all your persecutions and afflictions" (verse 4). His original Greek word for affliction is the very word that's elsewhere translated "tribulation" for the tribulation period, though here he's using it more generally for persecution at the present time.

Pretrib Void in the Book of Revelation

ered to him" right after a description of that revelation (2 Thess. 1:4–2:1)?

Above all, take the Book of Revelation. It contains by far the greatest amount of detail that we find anywhere in the New Testament about the tribulation and second coming. Furthermore, it was written by an apostle of the Christian church and addressed to seven local churches. In fact, chapters 2–3 of the book contain seven messages (one might almost say, epistles) to those churches. And it was probably written toward the end of the first century, making it the last or nearly last book of the New Testament to have been written. Here if anywhere, then, we'd expect to read a statement that Jesus will return before the tribulation, or a description that puts his return at that early point.

Posttrib Mass in the Book of Revelation

Such a statement and such a description are left out, however. Instead, we find a detailed description of Jesus' return after the tribulation. It is, in fact, the most detailed description of that event found anywhere in the New Testament:

> And I saw heaven opened, and behold, a white horse and the one sitting on it called "Faithful and True." And in righteousness he judges and makes war. And his eyes are like a flame of fire, and on his head are many crowns. He has a name inscribed that no one knows except he himself. And he is clothed with a garment dipped in blood, and his name is called "The Word of God." And the armies in heaven, clothed with fine linen, white and clean, were following him on white horses. And out of his mouth comes a sharp sword in order that he might strike the nations with it. And he

himself will shepherd them with an iron
rod, and he himself will tread the winepress of the wine of the anger of the wrath
of God the Almighty. And he has on his
garment and on his thigh a name inscribed, "King of kings and Lord of lords"
(19:11–16).

Preceding this passage is a description of
the fall of Babylon at the close of the tribulation, plus heavenly praise for that fall, and
following this passage is a description of the
slaughter at Armageddon. So there is no dis-
pute over the timing of this advent of Christ.
Unequivocally, it follows the tribulation.

Now why would John the seer spend so
much ink on describing Jesus' return after
the tribulation, but not a drop in describing
a return of Jesus before the tribulation, if
the earlier return is the main event that his
Christian audience should be looking for?
So far as that goes, why does John spend so
much ink on describing the tribulation—
fifteen chapters' worth (4–18)—if his Christian audience can't possibly enter the tribulation? It doesn't make sense; and sensi-
ble lay people shouldn't allow themselves
to be hoodwinked by esoteric evasions of
the obvious.

Posttrib Gathering

If we define the rapture strictly as a catching up, only one passage in the entire New
Testament describes it. That passage is 1
Thessalonians 4:13–18. If we broaden the
definition to include a gathering or reception, Matthew 24:31; Mark 13:27; John 14:1–
3; 2 Thessalonians 2:1; and Revelation
14:14–16 also come into the picture. Of
course, teachers of pretribulationism rule
out Matthew 24:31; Mark 13:27; and Revela-

tion 14:14–16 because these passages have posttrib settings. But the very necessity of ruling them out to maintain pretribulationism exposes a weakness: it is only the theory, not the data of the biblical text, that keeps anybody from understanding the gatherings in Matthew 24:31; Mark 13:27; and Revelation 14:14–16 as referring to the rapture.

The Scarcity of Rapture in the New Testament

And after those passages have been ruled out, what's left? Only John 14:1–3; 1 Thessalonians 4:13–18; and 2 Thessalonians 2:1. Teachers of pretribulationism regularly include 1 Corinthians 15:51–52, too; but there we don't read about a catching up, gathering, or reception—only about the resurrection of deceased believers and the translation of living ones. But even including this last passage, only four passages are left. In other words, the New Testament shows far more interest in Christ's coming as such than in the rapture of the church which occurs on that occasion. So nobody should demand an explicit statement to the effect that the *catching up* of the church will occur after the tribulation.

Pretrib No-Shows

The only passage that speaks of a catching up in connection with Christ's coming (1 Thess. 4:13–18) certainly doesn't say that this twofold event will occur before the tribulation. Nor does John 14:1–3; 2 Thessalonians 2:1; or 1 Corinthians 15:51–52 say "before the tribulation" or anything similar. In fact, no passage anywhere in the New Testament explicitly puts before the tribulation a single one of the constituent elements: coming of Christ, resurrection, translation, gathering, catching up, and reception of saints. Any of these would do, but none are forthcoming.

Yet the New Testament does tell us explicitly that Christ will come again after the tribulation, that saints will rise from the dead after the tribulation, and that the elect will be gathered after the tribulation—and Paul uses their being gathered synonymously with their being caught up (compare 1 Thess. 4:16–17 with 2 Thess. 2:1) and puts the translation of some together with the resurrection of others (1 Cor. 15:15–52). So where does the burden of proof lie? Obviously on the side of pretribulationism. Have teachers of this theory succeeded in carrying that burden? You judge. (What Jesus' coming and receiving the disciples means in John 14:1–3, and the time of his doing so, we'll take up later.)

Posttrib Shows

Teachers of pretribulationism complain that posttribulationists shouldn't saddle them with a burden of proof. But why not saddle them with it? Everybody agrees that the rapture occurs at the Lord's coming. First Thessalonians 4:13–18 says so explicitly. The New Testament also says explicitly that the Lord will come right after the tribulation, but never that he'll come before it.

The Pretrib Burden of Proof

Pretrib teachers respond that neither does the New Testament put the rapture right after the tribulation. Oh, but it does if you don't stop reading at the end of 1 Thessalonians 4 but read on into 1 Thessalonians 5 and 2 Thessalonians 1–2, as we've seen. Even if not, the New Testament joins the rapture to the Lord's coming, which it does put right after the tribulation, and Paul uses rapture synonymously with gathering, which the New Testament also puts right after the tribulation. So why don't teachers of pretribulationism shoulder their rightful

A Burden Too Heavy

burden of proof? Does their refusal betray a felt inability to sustain that burden?

An Early Posttrib Passage in Revelation

Another description of the second coming appears in the Book of Revelation long before 19:11–16, but like that later, very detailed one it refers to Jesus' return after the tribulation: "Behold, he is coming with the clouds, and every eye will see him, and those who pierced him. And all the tribes of the earth will wail because of him" (1:7). As pretribulationists agree, the descriptive phraseology, universal visibility, and judgmental purpose of this coming set it firmly in line with Jesus' coming after the tribulation according to Matthew 24:29–30; Mark 13:24–26; Luke 21:25–27; 2 Thessalonians 1:5–9; Revelation 19:11–16.

Indefinite Passages as Nonarguments

Of course, the New Testament contains many references to the second coming that lack a chronological setting; that is, the nearby events of the tribulation don't come into view at all. Pretrib teachers will sometimes seize on this fact to argue, "See, the New Testament does teach a coming of Christ unrelated to the tribulation and hence before the tribulation." This argument might have made a little sense if somewhere in the New Testament we could discover a definite statement that Jesus will return before the tribulation. But we don't find such a statement, so that tying the chronologically indefinite references to his return to a return that precedes the tribulation is like trying to use a bubble for an anchor.

How useless such an attempt is can be seen from taking several examples: Romans 13:1–2; Philippians 4:5; Hebrews 10:25; and James 5:8–9 all describe the Lord and his coming as "near." I choose these examples as the strongest that teachers of pretribulationism can provide, because nearness suggests to them an occurrence before the tribulation. The trouble is, elsewhere the language of nearness describes the return of Christ *after* the tribulation, his only return that is chronologically set by the New Testament—in other words, his only return at all (see Matt. 24:33; Mark 13:29; Luke 21:28; compare 1 Peter 4:7 and the nearness in John 2:13; 6:4; 7:2; 11:55 of Jewish festivals, events set on the calendar and therefore incapable of happening at any moment the way pretribulationism treats the nearness of Jesus' return for the church).

Posttrib Nearness

Besides, Paul writes in 2 Thessalonians 2:1–5 that during his stay with the Thessalonian Christians he described to them the Antichrist's rebellion and revelation as taking place before the Day of the Lord arrives. This description shows that in 1 Thessalonians 4:13–5:11 Paul doesn't think he needs to include the chronological setting of Jesus' return after the tribulation. So we must limit our thinking to the second coming *then,* not expand it unscripturally to include a second coming before the tribulation and thus make the later, undisputed return into what would properly be called a third coming.

Please, No Third Coming

Apparently to avoid the embarrassment of what amounts to a third coming in addition to the second coming, some teachers of pretribulationism have taken to talking about the rapture and the second coming—

The Unity of Rapture and Second Coming

the rapture occurring before the tribulation in their view, of course, and the second coming after the tribulation. But they can't get out of the embarrassment of two second comings, or a second coming plus a third one, quite so easily. For the only New Testament passage that describes the rapture as such—that is, as a catching up of Christians—starts with a statement about Jesus' *coming* at that time: "For the Lord himself will descend [or 'come down,' as the original Greek could equally well be translated] from heaven . . ." (1 Thess. 4:16–17). Furthermore, other passages that teachers of pretribulationism regularly interpret as pretribulational speak often of Jesus as coming: John 14:1–3; 1 Corinthians 16:22; 1 Thessalonians 2:19; 5:23; 2 Thessalonians 2:1; James 5:8; 1 John 2:28; Revelation 2:25.

Differentiating Translation from Rapture

Some teachers of pretribulationism have also taken to using "translation" as a synonym for "rapture." Apparently they are embarrassed by the presence of only one passage in the New Testament that speaks of a catching up of Christians at Jesus' coming, and they want to add to that minimal number by introducing passages which speak about the translation of Christians, as though that were equivalent to their rapture, or catching up.

Now it's true that we commonly speak about Enoch's and Elijah's translations to heaven (Gen. 5:24; 2 Kings 2:11; Heb. 11:5). But in a context of the second coming, "translation" has traditionally been used for the glorification of saints still living at the time, whose bodies won't need resurrection but will need immortalizing (Rom. 8:17; 1 Cor. 15:51–52; Phil. 3:20–21; 1 John

3:2; compare Romans 8:19 in its context of God's transforming the world of nature when Christians are revealed in their glorified state). And since the passages which talk about the translation of saints in the sense of their glorification or immortalization say nothing about being caught up or going to heaven, as in the cases of Enoch and Elijah, it's misleading to use those passages as if they were speaking about a rapture. This translation and the rapture will occur at the same time, of course, but so also will the second coming and the resurrection. These terms aren't all synonymous just because they all refer to elements in one overall event.

There's a pretrib argument that if 2 Thessalonians 2:1–4 promises relief from persecution at a posttrib rapture, comparatively few Christians will benefit, because most Christians will have gained such release by dying beforehand. But for the same reason, comparatively few Christians would be relieved from persecution at a *pre*trib rapture (even fewer than at a posttrib rapture, in fact, since the tribulation will see an increase in persecution); and nobody denies the translation of living saints, whenever it occurs, just because the majority of saints, including those in the first century to whom the promises of translation were originally written, will have died by then. So the pretrib argument aborts itself.

TESTING THE REST OF REVELATION

7

We've probed the Book of Revelation for what it has to say on watching for Jesus' return, the Day of the Lord, on the protection of believers from God's wrath, and also for the book's leaving out any return of Jesus before the tribulation. But the rest of Revelation has sparked a number of pretrib arguments. Let's put these arguments to the test. The examination will produce a grade of F by showing them to depend on faulty interpretations having no probative value.

In 1:19 Jesus tells John, "Write then the things that you have seen and the things that are and the things that are going to take place after these things." According to a pretrib argument, "the things that you have seen" consist of John's vision of Jesus in chapter 1. "The things that are" consist of the messages directed in chapters 2 and 3 to seven churches in Asia (not the continent of Asia, but a Roman province in what we now call Asia Minor or Turkey). "The things that are going to take place" consist of the tribu-

"After These Things" according to Pretribulationism

79

lation and following events as described in the remaining chapters. And since the things that are going to take place will do so "after these things," and since these earlier things consist of messages to the seven churches, the later things have nothing to do with the earlier things. In other words, the tribulation has nothing to do with the church.

A Shaky Assumption   At least a couple of weaknesses undermine this argument. First, it assumes that the seven churches represent the period or age of the whole church, so that the following things of the tribulation fall outside that period or age. Usually this assumption is accompanied by a chronologically successive interpretation of the church in Ephesus as representing the apostolic church, the church in Smyrna as representing the persecuted church of the second and third centuries, and so on to the church in Laodicea as representing the apostate church of the present and presumably last time.

Misgrading Church History   Naturally, the lengthening of church history has required some disconcerting readjustments of this interpretation. Also, the church in Thyatira gets higher marks from Jesus than pretribulationists usually give to the corrupt medieval church which it is supposed to represent. Conversely, the church of the Reformation is usually graded much higher than Jesus grades the church in Sardis, which supposedly represents it. And the "open door" that Jesus gives the church in Philadelphia (3:8) seems not to stand for modern missionary work, as in more recent church history (compare 1 Cor. 16:9; 2 Cor. 2:12; Col. 4:3), but for access into the messianic kingdom, as intimated by mention of "the key of David" (3:7; compare and contrast Isa. 22:22–23; Matt. 25:10; Luke 13:24–25; Acts 14:27). To the extent that they represent other churches at all, then, the seven churches in Revelation 2–3 would seem to represent different kinds of churches that have coexisted throughout the church age, not different eras within the church age.

Could it still be, though, that the seven churches stand collectively for the church age as a whole, so that the tribulation, which belongs to the following things, excludes the church? The error in thinking so still comes in treating the seven churches as representative of an age. The churches are what they are—churches, not a period of time. If you were to take "the things that are" (present tense) as standing for the current age of the church, what age would "the things that you have seen" (past tense) stand for? The vision of Jesus that John had just seen hardly represents an age prior to that of the church. In fact, John saw that vision right within the church age, for that age had gotten under way decades earlier. Well, if John's past vision of Jesus is compatible with the church age, so also John's future visions of the tribulation will be compatible with the church age.

The Seven Churches as Churches, Not an Age

Which brings us to a second and even more damaging weakness in the pretrib argument. It's an assumption that the past, present, and future tenses ("have seen," "are," and "are going to take place") have to do with the *fulfilment* of John's visions, so that "after these things" means that future visions of the tribulation can't be fulfilled till later than the supposed fulfilment of the

The Past, Present, and Future of John's Personal Experiences, Not of Prophetic Fulfilment

present vision concerning churches. But elsewhere in the Book of Revelation, "after these things" almost always refers to John's *personal experiences* in receiving one vision after another, as in the statements, "After these things I looked [or 'saw'] . . ." (4:1a; 7:9; 15:5; 18:1; compare 7:1) and "After these things I heard . . ." (19:1), and to the happening of events after John's experiences ("the things that must take place after these things," that is, after what happened to John in his seeing of the initial vision— 4:1b). Otherwise the phrase refers to a transition from one part of a vision to another: to the second and third woes as coming "after these things" of the first woe, which John has just seen (9:12), and to the loosing of Satan "after these things" of being bound for a thousand years and thrown into the abyss, which again John has just seen (20:3).

No Dispensational Shifts In none of these other instances does the phrase refer to a dispensational shift in the fulfilment of John's visions, not even in the last instance, for the loosing of Satan doesn't yet start the new age of eternal bliss. Instead, it leads to the unsuccessful rebellion of Gog and Magog against the millennial rule of Christ and the saints. So in 1:19 "the things that are going to take place after these things" doesn't mean that the events of the tribulation are going to take place in world history after the age of the church, but that they're going to take place in John's seeing of later visions once he has finished seeing the present one.

Past and Present in a Single Vision Furthermore, John saw Jesus ("the things that you have seen") and received from him messages for the seven churches ("the things that are") in one and the same vision, not in different visions, one past and one present. And at the time of Jesus' speaking in 1:19, John hadn't yet received the messages of chapters 2–3. Consequently, we shouldn't accept the pretrib equation of those messages with the things that Jesus said were already present at the time he was speaking.

At this point teachers of pretribulationism try another argument: since the word "church" appears nineteen times in chapters 1–3 but never in chapters 4–18, which describe the tribulation, the church must be absent from earth during that period. This argument depends on several oversights. First, a failure to notice that all appearances of "church" in chapters 1–3, plus a final appearance in 22:16, carry the sense of particular local churches in the restricted area of a Roman province, whereas descriptions of the tribulation in chapters 4–18 have to do at least with the whole Roman Empire, so that general references to the saints become more appropriate.

Provincial Churches and Imperial Saints

Second, a failure to notice that "church" doesn't appear in John's descriptions of heavenly scenes, which occupy a good deal of space in chapters 4–18, any more than it appears in John's descriptions of earthly scenes (for the heavenly scenes, see 4:1–5:14; 7:9–8:5; 11:15–12:17; 14:1–5; 15:1–8, to which should be added 19:1–10, because the description of Christ's coming after the tribulation doesn't begin till 19:11). "What's good for the goose is good for the gander": if the absence of "church" from earthly scenes were to imply an absence of the church down here, then the absence of

The Absence of "Church" from Heavenly as well as Earthly Scenes

"church" from heavenly scenes would imply an absence of the church up there. But few teachers of pretribulationism grant an absence of the church from heaven as well as from earth. Such a double absence would force them to put the church in space during the tribulation, and they would lose their understanding of passages such as John 14:1–3 (Jesus' taking believers at a pretrib rapture to be with him in his Father's *heavenly* house); Revelation 4:1 (John's going up *to heaven* as symbolic of the church's rapture), and Revelation 4:4, 10–11; 5:8–12 (the twenty-four elders *in heaven* as representing a just-raptured church).

The Absence of "Church" from Christ's Coming with the Church and from Supposedly Pretrib Passages

Third, a failure to notice that in the description of Christ's coming after the tribulation (19:11–16), "church" doesn't appear. Yet in the pretrib scheme, that coming is supposed to be a coming *with* the church as distinct from an earlier coming *for* the church. If the absence of "church" from the description of Jesus' return after the tribulation doesn't necessitate the church's absence from that return, neither does the absence of "church" from descriptions of the tribulation necessitate an absence of the church from the tribulation. For that matter, the word "church" never appears in any of the New Testament passages cited by teachers of pretribulationism as referring to a pretrib rapture (outstandingly, John 14:1–3; 1 Cor. 15:51–52; 1 Thess. 4:13–18; Titus 2:11–14; compare the absence of "church" from Mark, Luke, John, 2 Timothy, Titus, 1 Peter, 2 Peter, 1 John, 2 John, and Jude, and even from Romans 1–15: it would take a brave soul to try disengaging from the church all these parts of the New Testament).

Fourth, a failure to notice that since no passage of Scripture explicitly puts a return of Christ for the church before the tribulation (otherwise there'd be no debate), readers of Revelation should naturally presume that expressions which are used to identify and describe believers living on earth during the tribulation refer to the last generation of the church. After all, elsewhere in the New Testament these expressions refer to members of the church: "saints" (see especially 13:7, 10, plus numerous other instances both in Revelation and in the Book of Acts and the Epistles), "witnesses" (11:3; 17:6; compare Acts 1:8; 13:31), God's "people" (18:4; compare 2 Cor. 6:16; also Titus 2:14), God's "servants" (7:3; 19:2, 5; compare 1:1; 2:20; Acts 2:18; 4:29; 16:17). The argument isn't that such expressions *must* refer to members of the church; rather, that in the absence of contrary indications they *naturally* do.

The Church as Saints, Witnesses, God's People, and God's Servants

Well, then, if the absence of "church" from Revelation 4–18 doesn't prove the rapture of Christians to heaven before the tribulation, maybe John's going up to heaven in 4:1–2 does. He writes, "After these things I looked, and behold, an open door in heaven, and the first voice that I heard, speaking with me like a trumpet and saying, 'Come up here and I will show you the things that must take place after these things.' Immediately I was in the Spirit and, behold, a throne situated in heaven. . . ." The text doesn't say that John was "caught up," but his being told to come up and his suddenly being there are good enough. As

John's Going Up

The Two Witnesses' Going Up Posttrib

an apostle, mightn't John represent the whole church in a pretrib rapture?

Hardly. In the first place, why should John's going up to heaven represent a pretrib rapture any more than the going up to heaven of the two witnesses in 11:11–12 represents a posttrib rapture? The two witnesses' going up occurs after the trampling of the holy city during the second half of the tribulation. And in addition to the going up itself, the resurrection of the two witnesses and "the cloud" in which they go up parallel Paul's description of the church's rapture "in clouds" after deceased Christians "rise first" (1 Thess. 4:16–17) much more closely than the going up of John does.

Going Up for Seeing a Vision

Second, the phrase "in the Spirit" at 4:1–2 indicates that John's going up has the purpose merely of showing him another vision, just as in 1:10 and 17:3 the same phrase indicates a visionary state. We don't find the phrase in connection with the two witnesses' going up at 11:11–12. That passage predicts an event rather than narrating a past experience of John. By contrast, the presence of the phrase in 4:1–2 points to such an experience as opposed to the prediction of an event.

John's Commutings Between Heaven and Earth

Third, John is back on earth in 10:1 ("And I saw another strong angel coming down from heaven"), 8 ("And the voice that I had heard from heaven spoke to me again, saying, 'Go, take the scroll that is open in the hand of the angel who is standing on the sea and on the earth'"); 11:1 (". . . saying [to me], 'Get up and measure the temple' [whose court and city will be trampled by the nations according to the next verse, so that the earthly temple is in view; compare

12:18–13:1]"); 17:3 ("And he carried me away in the Spirit into a wilderness"); and 18:1 ("After these things I saw another angel coming down from heaven"). In between these earthly settings, John often finds himself in heaven again for the seeing of other visions. Now if his spatial location represents that of the Christian church, as would be the case if his going up to heaven in 4:1–2 represents a pretrib rapture, then the church will have to commute back and forth between heaven and earth a number of times during the tribulation—an absurd idea that nobody holds, least of all teachers of pretribulationism.

Let's give pretribulationism another try. If John's going up to heaven in 4:1–2 doesn't represent a pretrib rapture of the church, might the twenty-four elders he sees in heaven on his arrival represent the church as raptured before the tribulation? That they do is highly speculative. It's not even sure that the elders are human beings such as might represent the church well. Both in their nearness to God's throne and in their activity of leading heavenly worship, they are closely associated with "four living creatures," a special class of angelic beings (4:4–11; 5:6, 8–14; 7:11–12; 14:3; 19:4). Two of the elders interact with John as his guides and interpreters (5:5; 7:13–17) just as some angels do (17:1–18; 19:9–10 with 18:21; 21:9–11; compare 10:8–11:3). The elders are distinguished from redeemed human beings (see especially 14:1–4, but also compare 11:16–18; 19:5 and the best manuscripts in 5:9–10, which have "them" rather than "us" for the saints, though sometimes people do refer to themselves in the third person, as in

The Speculativeness of Churchly Elders and the Possibility of Angelic Elders

Exod. 15:13, 16–17). The elders wear crowns as human beings may do (2:10; 3:11), but beings other than humans also wear crowns (9:7; 12:3), so that crown-wearing doesn't imply humanity.

Crowns and Robes as Not Implying Rapture, Judgment, and Reward

Despite the promise of crowns and white robes for victorious Christians in 2:10; 3:4–5, the crowns and white robes that John sees the elders wearing don't imply the elders' recent rapture, quick judgment, and present reward any more than crown-wearing implies humanity. Judgment and reward are reserved for a later time, the seventh trumpet, which we have seen takes us to the coming of Christ after the tribulation (11:18). And white robes are worn by the souls of martyrs not yet resurrected, much less raptured (6:9–11; compare 20:4–5), and even by Christians still living on earth (3:18).

Conclusion: nothing in Revelation 4 proves that the twenty-four elders have recently gone up to heaven, or even that they originated on earth at an earlier time. More generally, then, we can also say that nothing in the chapter provides evidence convincing us to think of the twenty-four elders as representing a just-raptured church.

Unsupported Speculations about the 144,000

But what about the 144,000? Well, what about them? They show up in Revelation 7:1–8; 14:1–5. Nothing in those passages says that they'll replace Christians as preachers of the gospel during the tribulation—a view largely forced on teachers of pretribulationism because they have Christians gone by that time yet, as discussed earlier, the scriptural text makes clear that many, many saved people will be on earth and come out of the tribulation (see especially 7:9–17). How will these people be saved? Through the evangelistic efforts of the 144,000, say those same teachers of pretribulationism, since according to them the church's rapture will have left a vacuum of gospel-preaching. How then will the 144,000 be saved? Oh, maybe through reading the Bible or through noting the disappearance of Christians at a pretrib rapture. So they say again.

But look for yourself. There's nothing like those answers in the biblical text. Interpretation has turned into imagination. And who's to say, anyway, that Christians couldn't live on earth at the same time as the 144,000, and even preach the gospel at the same time they do—*if* they do?

Who are the 144,000? Pretribulationism takes them to be not only evangelists who replace the supposedly just-raptured church, but also male celibates who because of their bachelorhood can and do devote themselves full-time to evangelism and therefore succeed at it outstandingly. Presumably the benefits of bachelorhood are enough to make up for a withdrawal of the Holy Spirit such as pretribulationism sees in 2 Thessalonians 2:6–7. Not only male celibates, though—also Jews or, more accurately, Israelites, 12,000 from each of the twelve tribes of Israel, so that they stand in some contrast to their innumerable converts from every nation and all tribes and peoples and tongues, according to the pretrib understanding of 7:9–17.

The text does describe the 144,000 as "virgins" in whose mouth "no lie was found," so that "they are blameless" (14:4–5). But virginity doesn't necessarily refer to cel-

God-Worshippers, Not Bachelors

ibacy and bachelorhood. It may refer instead to avoidance of idolatry and of the cultic prostitution associated with idolatry, as in 2 Corinthians 11:2, where Paul writes of his desire to present the Christians at Corinth—certainly not just celibate bachelors among them—"as a pure virgin to Christ" (compare and contrast James 4:4; 2 Kings 19:21; Jer. 18:13–17; Lam. 2:13; Ezek. 23:1–49; Amos 5:2). In particular, the virginity of the 144,000 likely refers, not to celibacy in bachelorhood, but to refusal to practice the idolatry of worshipping the Beast and of engaging in the associated sexual perversions of the harlot Babylon, for the context in Revelation deals with these topics, not with the topic of unmarried sexual purity (see the immediately preceding chapter 13 and the immediately following 14:6–13; also 15:2; 16:2; 17:1–19:4 and, for the pure bride and wife of the Lamb, 19:5–10; 20:4; 21:2, 9; 22:17).

The writing of God the Father's name on the foreheads of the 144,000 (14:1)—also called "the seal of the living God" (7:2; see, too, 7:3; 9:4)—marks the 144,000 as worshippers of God in contrast to worshippers of the Beast, whose mark "666" brands those worshippers as his idolaters (13:1–18). The finding of "no lie" in the mouth of the 144,000 portrays them as those who hold "the testimony of Jesus" (6:9; 12:11, 17; 19:10; 20:4) rather than being deceived by "the false prophet" and thus confessing and worshipping the Beast (13:11–18; 16:13; 19:20; 20:10; note also the pairing of idolaters and liars in 21:8; compare 21:27; 22:15). Once again, then, the 144,000 look like faithful worshippers of God and the

Lamb, not like Jewish bachelors whose evangelistic energies are enhanced by sexual abstinence.

But the listing of the 144,000 as coming 12,000 a shot from each of the twelve tribes of Israel (7:4–8) at least portrays them as Jews, Israelites, or, in contemporary lingo, Israelis—yes? No, probably not. Take the frequency of the number 12 in the Book of Revelation. We read about a crown of twelve stars (12:1), a city with twelve gates consisting of twelve pearls and having twelve angels and the inscribed names of the twelve tribes of Israel (21:12, 21), with twelve foundations consisting of twelve other gems and having on them the names of the twelve apostles (21:14, 19–20), and with a river on both sides of which grow specimens of the tree of life bearing twelve crops of fruit, one for each of the twelve months of the year (22:2). Moreover, the city is 12,000 stadia long, wide, and high, so that being cube-shaped—like the Holy of holies, the dwelling place of God among his people in the Old Testament—its 12 edges being multiplied by 12,000 come to 144,000 (21:16). And its walls are 144, that is 12 x 12, cubits high (21:17). Since this city, the New Jerusalem, comprises Christian believers in their final destiny, it begins to look as though the 144,000 represent them, the church as new Israel—12 for the number of God's people, squared to emphasize completeness, and then multiplied by 1,000 to emphasize how many they are.

The Church Portrayed as New Israel

Supporting this view of the 144,000 is the fact that elsewhere in the Book of Revelation, members of the seven churches are described in terms reminiscent of Israel in

Christians Described as New Israelites

the Old Testament (see 1:6 with Exod. 19:6 on royal priesthood, 2:14 with Num. 25:1–18; 31:16 on eating idol-meat and fornicating, and 2:20 with 1 Kings 16:31; 2 Kings 9:22 on the same activities in connection with Jezebel), and they are given promises in Old Testament terms (see 2:7 with Gen. 2:9; 3:3, 22, 24 on eating from the tree of life; also 2:17 with Exod. 16:31–36 on eating manna, 2:26 with Ps. 2:8–9 on exercising authority over the nations, 3:5 with Ps. 69:28 on being written in the book of life, and 3:12 with many Old Testament passages concerning Jerusalem and the temple). Of course, we can think again of the numerous parallels between tribulational plagues and the plagues on Egypt, and between the redemption of New Testament saints and the redemption of Israel from Egypt.

Difference and Sameness in Hearing and Seeing

Capping this evidence is another consideration. In his initial vision of the 144,000 John only *heard* about them. When he looked to *see* them, he saw a large and innumerable throng of the redeemed from every nation and all tribes and peoples and tongues (7:4, 9). Earlier we find a similar phenomenon: John *heard* about "the Lion of the tribe of Judah," but he *saw* "a Lamb" (5:5–6). Since the Lion *is* the Lamb, both animals representing Jesus, the 144,000 *are* the multitude of redeemed, both groups representing the church.

The 144,000 as the Church's Last Generation

Just as the contrasts between lion and lamb are only apparent, so also the contrasts between 144,000 Israelites and an innumerable, multinational throng of the redeemed are only apparent. Dig deeper—there's no difference. The number 144,000 doesn't set a numerical limit. It signifies innumerability. The listing of twelve tribes doesn't set an ethnic limit. It signifies a theological status. That is to say, the 144,000 don't replace the church on earth during the tribulation. They *are* the church on earth during the tribulation. If anyone casts suspicion on this interpretation because it treats John's language as symbolic rather than literal, then let that person take literally Jesus' being both a lion and a lamb—at the same time, no less!

Though not always, sometimes in pretribulationism the marriage supper of the Lamb, mentioned in 19:6–10, is thought to take place in heaven while the tribulation takes place on earth. Since the church is the bride, the Lamb's wife, naturally the church will have to be in heaven for that supper. And to get there it will need to have been raptured before the tribulation.

The Marriage Supper as Neither Heavenly Nor Tribulational

This argument lacks weight, however, because the Book of Revelation does not locate the marriage supper of the Lamb in heaven or the tribulation. On the contrary, Revelation saves the supper for mention not until the verge of Jesus' coming to earth after the tribulation, the description of which coming follows immediately in 19:11–16. The statement that the marriage supper "has come" (19:7) doesn't mean that it has already taken place. Rather, the time for it has now arrived, at Jesus' posttribulational advent, just as the statement in 6:17 that the great day of God's and the Lamb's wrath "has come" means that its time has arrived (the wicked are fleeing in the face of it), not that it arrived some time earlier. "Strike one!" against the marriage supper of the Lamb as an argument for pretribulationism.

Earthly Not Heavenly Preparation

Against the pretrib argument that it will take some time for the church as Christ's bride to prepare herself for the marriage supper (19:7 says that she "has prepared herself"), we should ask why this preparation has to take place in heaven by virtue of a prior rapture. Elsewhere in the New Testament, such preparation for the second coming is to take place on earth through godly living and watchful expectancy (Matt. 24:44: "On account of this, you also be prepared . . . ," at the close of a parable about the second coming). And right here, Revelation 19:8 interprets the preparation as "the righteous deeds of the saints." These deeds were hardly done in heaven! "Strike two!" against the marriage supper of the Lamb as an argument for pretribulationism.

The Lateness of the Marriage Supper

But some pretrib teachers go on to argue that since ancient Semitic custom had a groom fetch his bride from her home and take her to his home, the marriage supper of the Lamb implies that Jesus came earlier—that is, before the tribulation—to fetch his bride the church from her home on earth, and took her to his home in heaven, where the marriage supper was held during the tribulation. Strange, then, that the marriage supper has been saved for mention in immediate association with what everybody acknowledges to be Jesus' coming after the tribulation.

The Nonmention of Bride-Fetching

Furthermore, if a purported pretrib coming to fetch the church to heaven is supposed to reflect the ancient Semitic custom of a groom's fetching the bride to his home, what is Jesus' taking the church

with him back to earth right after the marriage supper, and for a thousand years,
supposed to reflect? An ancient Semitic
custom of the groom's taking his bride
back to *her* home to live with her there for
a long time? The pretrib reasoning gets itself in a pickle by injecting a marriage custom that isn't even mentioned in the biblical text at hand, and then giving that
custom argumentative weight of an alle-
gorical sort but not carrying out the alle-
gory consistently. In fact, our ignorance of
ancient Semitic marriage customs exceeds
our knowledge. And what knowledge we
do have shows considerable variation in
those customs.

In a passage that does speak of Jesus' return in terms of a groom's coming—that is,
Matthew 25:1–13, which contains the parable of ten virgins—it isn't the fetched
bride who represents the church. It's the
virgins. The bride isn't even mentioned. So
no fetching is mentioned, either. Since the
virgins represent the church on earth,
their awaiting his coming has to do with a
coming to earth for a marriage supper
down here. They're not waiting in heaven
for him to bring his bride for a marriage
supper up there. And since they go out to
meet him only to escort him right back to
where they were, as in a posttrib catching
up of the church from the earth to meet
the Lord in the air and escort him right
back to earth rather than his making a U-
turn to take the church to heaven—well,
"Strike three!" and "Out!" for the marriage
supper of the Lamb as an argument for
pretribulationism.

**The Army of
Deceased
Saints Already
in Heaven**

"The armies in heaven" follow Jesus at his return to earth after the tribulation (19:14). The clothing of this army "in fine linen, white and clean" supports their identification with the church, the Lamb's bride, who is clothed in "fine linen, bright and clean" (19:8). If then the church constitutes the army, it is sometimes argued, a pretrib rapture must have taken them to heaven.

But a large proportion of the church consists of deceased saints already in heaven (see, for example, the souls of martyrs under the heavenly altar in 6:9–11, and the blessing on those "who are dying in the Lord" at 14:13). As the most prominent and well-respected of all pretrib teachers has himself written, "He [Jesus] will bring the souls of Christians who have died with Him . . . . the body will be resurrected and the soul will reenter the body" (and see Rev. 6:9–11 for the clothing of these souls prior to the resurrection).[1] There's also the possibility that, as often, "heaven" means "sky," to which living saints have just been raptured in accordance with the harvest reaped in 14:14–16 by "one like a son of man sitting on a white cloud" (see 6:13–14; 8:10; 9:1; 11:6; 12:4; 16:21 for particularly clear examples of "heaven" in the sense of "sky").

**The Posttrib
Resurrection
of Saints**

Revelation 20:4–6 speaks about a resurrection of saints that will take place after the tribulation and before the millennium.

1. John F. Walvoord, "1 Thessalonians 4: A Central Rapture Passage," in *When the Trumpet Sounds*, ed. Thomas Ice and Timothy Demy (Eugene, Oreg.: Harvest House, 1995) 256.

Some teachers of pretribulationism say that the wording of this passage limits the resurrection to saints who died by martyrdom during the tribulation. From that standpoint these teachers then argue that another resurrection must have taken place before the tribulation, for otherwise the saints who died before the tribulation remain unresurrected—yet 1 Thessalonians 4:16–17 puts their resurrection at the Lord's coming and rapture of the church.

Those who argue this way are inconsistent, though, for they themselves locate the resurrection of Old Testament saints at the time of Revelation 20:4–6. (They have to, in their own terms, because to locate the resurrection of Old Testament saints before the tribulation would be to confuse Israel and the church.) Well, if Old Testament saints can rise from the dead right after the tribulation even though their resurrection isn't mentioned in Revelation 20:4–6, why not Christians who died before the tribulation, too, even though their resurrection isn't mentioned in Revelation 20:4–6?

More important than this inconsistency in the pretrib argument is the question whether the wording of Revelation 20:4–6 really does limit the resurrection spoken about there to saints who died by martyrdom during the tribulation. John does make special mention of those martyrs to encourage Christians who face persecution. But before mentioning them in particular, he speaks in general about "they" who will sit on thrones (to rule with Christ for a thousand years, as John says later). Furthermore, the phrase "the first resurrection" seems more general than allowed by a limitation to those who died as martyrs during the tribulation. And the description of those who are resurrected here as reigning with Christ matches earlier descriptions of true Christians in general as reigning with him (2:26; 3:21; 5:10; see also Matt. 19:28; 1 Cor. 6:2–3).

So the whole argument breaks down. More than that, the similarity to those earlier descriptions actually favors that the same people are in view, that is, Christians, members of the church, so that their resurrection will occur after the tribulation according to Revelation 20:4–6, not beforehand. And if the resurrection of deceased Christians will occur after the tribulation, so also will their rapture along with that of those still living when the Lord returns.

The Rapture in Terms of a Posttrib Harvest

Sometimes it's asked why the Book of Revelation doesn't describe the rapture as such in conjunction with Jesus' return after the tribulation if the rapture will in fact occur at that coming. In this way the force of the argument that the book doesn't describe a pretrib coming of Christ is thought to be diminished. But consider the first of the two harvests in 14:14–20. "One like a son of man"—exactly the phrase that identifies Jesus in 1:13—reaps this harvest (compare John 5:27). He is sitting "on a white cloud" in accordance with Jesus' coming "with the clouds" after the tribulation, when "every eye will see him, even those who pierced him, and all the tribes of the earth will wail because of him" (1:7; see also Dan. 7:13; Matt. 24:30; 26:64; Mark 13:26; 14:62; Luke 21:27; Acts 1:9–11; 1 Thess. 4:16–17). In contrast with the subsequent grape-gathering and winepress-

treading, which are expressly said to sym-
bolize the infliction of "God's wrath," the
cloud-sitting Jesus reaps a harvest of grain
(see Paul's comparison of the resurrection
and translation of Christians to a grain harvest—1 Cor. 15:23, 35–49).

The introduction of this grain harvest
with a blessing on "the ones dying in the
Lord" (14:13) suits the resurrection of
Christians at the rapture (again see 1 Thess.
4:16–17). And the situation of this blessing
and harvest between announcements of
God's judgment, the fall of Babylon, and
God's wrath (14:6–12) and descriptions of
Babylon's fall, the seven last plagues of
God's wrath, and the Battle of Armageddon
(14:17–19:4) locates the grain harvest, representing rapture, at Jesus' return after the
tribulation. The Book of Revelation isn't so
silent on a posttrib rapture after all, just as
it isn't silent on Christ's coming after the
tribulation (19:11–16) or on the resurrection of saints after the tribulation (20:4–
6)—that is, on all the essential elements
that pretribulationism puts before the tribulation without support from the Book of
Revelation.

SIDEBAR

Some have denied the identification with
Jesus of the "one like a son of man" who sits
"on the white cloud" and reaps a harvest of
grain in 14:14–16. Their reason: an angel
wouldn't tell Jesus to reap as the angel in
this vision tells the one like a son of man to
reap. But the angel's coming "out of the
temple" indicates that he is merely relaying
a message from God the Father, and the

**Jesus as One
Like a Son of
Man**

The Difference between Weeding and Winepressing

writings of John regularly portray Jesus as doing his Father's will (see, for example, John 4:34; 5:30; 6:38).

Some have also resisted identifying the grain harvest in 14:14–16 with the rapture. They reason that in 14:17–20 the judgmental gathering and winepress-treading follow the grain harvest, whereas in Matthew 13:24–30, 36–43 the judgmental harvest of weeds precedes the grain harvest of saints. No problem: the parable in Matthew deals with weeding false disciples out of God's kingdom, whereas Revelation deals with the Battle of Armageddon—quite a different kettle of fish. If there were a real problem, it would be worse for pretribulationism, because according to that view—whatever the interpretation of 14:14–16—the harvest of saints at a rapture comes a full seven years or more before the judgmental harvest at Armageddon.

It isn't essential to posttribulationism that the twenty-four elders be angelic rather than human, but it has been argued from the pretrib standpoint that they can't be angelic because nowhere else in the Bible are angels said to sit. They stand, fly, and hover, but they don't sit. Yet the twenty-four elders do sit, as do also the overcomers, or true Christians, in Revelation 3:21: "The one who overcomes—to that one I will grant to sit with me on my throne as I, too, overcame and sat with my Father on his throne." Therefore the elders do not equate with angels but represent the church, raptured just before the tribulation. So say the teachers of pretribulationism.

Sitting Angels

One is tempted to respond in their style and ask why then the elders are sitting on their own thrones rather than on the throne of Jesus and his Father, as overcoming Christians are said to do. More importantly and validly, though, it's outright false that elsewhere in the Bible angels never sit. An angel of the Lord sits on the stone that he has rolled away from Jesus' empty tomb, for example. Nor can he be equated with Jesus, for he says concerning Jesus, "He is not here. . . . he is going ahead of you into Galilee" (Matt. 28:2, 6–7; see also Mark 16:5 and Judg. 6:11).

Stadia, Not Miles; Cubits, Not Yards

At Revelation 21:16 some contemporary English translations have "1,500 miles" instead of "12,000 stadia." The change from ancient stadia to modern miles obscures the symbolism of 12,000. At 21:17 some contemporary English translations likewise have "72 yards" instead of "144 cubits." The change from ancient cubits to modern yards likewise obscures the symbolism of 144.

Hinting at a Slippery Slope

Often, teachers of pretribulationism charge that posttribulationism rests on a nonliteral and therefore mistaken interpretation of Scripture, and claim that a consistently literal and therefore correct interpretation of Scripture yields a pretrib result. With talk of a "slippery slope," some teachers of pretribulationism then hint darkly that the supposed nonliteralism of posttribulationists leads to a denial that Jesus will reign with the saints on earth for a thousand years following his return. And eventually and disastrously to a theological liberalism that is capable of treating Jesus' resurrection, for example, solely as a religious symbol rather than as a theologically significant historical event.

Posttrib Literalism   Never mind that many of the most godly and effective defenders of historic Christian orthodoxy haven't believed that the Bible teaches an earthly kingdom following Jesus' return and lasting a thousand years (though I agree with pretribulationists that those defenders have gone wrong on the millennial issue). Anybody who seriously believes that the Antichrist will appear, lead a rebellion against God, and persecute the church, and believes that Jesus will return after the tribulation during which those events occur—such a posttribulationist can hardly be accused of taking the Bible so loosely as to be sliding down a slippery slope into theological liberalism. An end to contrary innuendoes!

Pretrib Nonliteralism   As a matter of fact, though, teachers of pretribulationism themselves often adopt nonliteral interpretations and disagree among themselves on what should be taken as literal and what should be taken as figurative or symbolic. Some of them adopt a symbolic interpretation of the last earthquake and celestial phenomena, for example. Many and perhaps most of them likewise adopt a symbolic interpretation of Babylon in the Book of Revelation. During their better moments they explicitly allow that some biblical language, like some language outside the Bible, isn't intended to be taken literally while other such language is so intended. The trick is to decide the intended meaning case by case, passage by passage, by paying attention to contexts and showing sensitivity to differences in kinds of literature. You expect more figures of speech in poetry, more literalism in prose, greater symbolism in an apocalyptic vision, less in a historical report, and so on.

Literalism doesn't always equate with truth. The LORD's turning the earth upside down according to the King James Version of Isaiah 24:1 doesn't have to mean that what is now the north pole used to be the south pole, and vice versa (whatever the scientific truth of the matter), as I once heard a prominent and much-published teacher of pretribulationism solemnly declare. Human language is supple; and the Bible, inspired by the Holy Spirit as it is, communicates to us in human language and should be understood accordingly.

Orthodox Symbolism

GATHERED, CAUGHT UP 8

What's expressed figuratively as the reaping of a harvest in Revelation 14:14–16 is expressed literally as a gathering in Matthew 24:31; Mark 13:27; 2 Thessalonians 2:1. The last of these passages carries the following phraseology: "concerning the coming of our Lord Jesus Christ and our being gathered together to him." Since Paul's "our" includes the church in Thessalonica along with him, the phraseology has to do with the church's rapture at the second coming. But at what second coming? One before the tribulation?

Rapture as Gathering

No, because Paul has just described Jesus' "revelation from heaven with his mighty angels in flaming fire, rendering vengeance on those who do not know God and do not obey the gospel"—hardly the description of a pretrib coming and rapture (2 Thess. 1:7–12). Also because Paul immediately goes on to say that the Day of the Lord won't arrive unless the Antichrist's rebellion and revelation come first (2 Thess. 2:3–

Posttrib Gathering in Paul

4), and in 1 Thessalonians 5:1–11 Paul has said to watch for the Day of the Lord, which because Christians are to watch for it must be the occasion of "the coming of the Lord" when they "will be caught up . . . to meet the Lord in the air" (1 Thess. 4:13–18). And finally because a few verses later Paul identifies the coming of the Lord Jesus as one at which "he will destroy" the Antichrist "with the breath of his mouth" (2 Thess. 2:8).

Posttrib Gathering in Jesus

Just as Paul puts the catching up or gathering of Christians after the career of the Antichrist—that is, after the tribulation—so Jesus puts the gathering of the elect at his coming "immediately after the tribulation of those days" (Matt. 24:21–31; see also Mark 13:24–27). To get around the parallel between the gathering that Jesus talks about and the one that Paul writes about, teachers of pretribulationism commonly interpret Jesus as talking about a posttrib gathering of Jews who still live outside the land of Israel back into that land, and Paul as writing about a pretrib gathering of Christians by way of their being caught up to meet the Lord in the air. Two different gatherings, in other words—different times, different people, different purposes, even different directions (up into the air for Christians, horizontally across the face of the earth for returning Jews).

Not a Jewish Gathering

But these distinctions don't grow out of the scriptural text. They're made only because the theory of pretribulationism requires them. After all, since Paul interprets the gathering of Christians as a catching up, it makes sense for us to interpret the gathering of the elect that Jesus talked about as a catching up. In fact, Paul's use of gathering, the same terminology that Jesus used, suggests that Paul borrows it from Jesus and interprets it himself as a catching up. And since Jesus has just spoken about a preaching of the gospel "to all nations" (Mark 13:10; see also Matt 24:14), there's no reason to think of dispersed Jews as "the elect" who are gathered—rather, the multi-national church, whom Paul likewise calls "the elect" (Rom. 8:33; 16:13; Col. 3:12; 2 Tim. 2:10; Titus 1:1; compare the verb "elect" in 1 Cor. 1:27, 28; Eph. 1:4).

Yet again, the distinctions made in pretribulationism between different gatherings overlook that Paul's putting the gathering at the Day of the Lord after the Antichrist's rebellion and revelation doesn't diverge from Jesus' placement of the gathering, but matches it exactly. Further supporting the parallel is the mention of clouds and a trumpet in both Matthew 24:30–31 and 1 Thessalonians 4:16–17. In 1 Corinthians 15:52, similarly, Paul puts the resurrection and translation of Christians "at the last trumpet."

Equation, Not Differentiation

In these same passages Jesus mentions angels, Paul only an archangel. But Paul also mentions angels in the plural when describing the Lord's coming to give Christians relief from persecution (2 Thess. 1:7), so that what might look at first like a slight but telltale distinction in number turns out to differentiate not at all between pre- and posttrib comings and gatherings. Of course, Jesus says that his *angels* will gather the elect (Matt. 24:31), and Paul doesn't. But then Paul doesn't identify anyone else as gathering or catching up Christians, either. So for him it might as well be angels. Besides, according to Mark 13:27, which parallels Matthew 24:31, it is Jesus who will gather his elect—obviously through the agency of angels, since he sends them. So even if Paul had said that Jesus will gather or catch up Christians, it would remain as possible in Paul's writings as in Jesus' words that angels act as agents in carrying out the task.

We should conclude, then, that the gathering of the elect at Jesus' return after the tribulation equates with the gathering of Christians to the Lord at his coming after the Antichrist's rebellion and revelation, and that these two gatherings equate in turn with the catching up of Christians when the Day of the Lord arrives and he descends to earth. But why are Christians caught up to meet him in the air if he keeps coming down rather than taking them to heaven? Why don't they wait for him until he arrives on earth?

Down and Up versus Up and Down

Of course, the same sort of question could be asked from the other side: In pretribulationism, why does the Lord come down to take Christians to heaven? Why don't they go up all the way without him, as Enoch, Elijah, Paul, and John did (see Gen. 5:24; 2 Kings 2:1–12; 2 Cor. 12:1–4; Rev. 4:1–2)? Why doesn't Jesus wait for Christians until they arrive in heaven? So long as there's a meeting in the air, somebody has to turn around and go back, either Jesus back to heaven, as in pretribulationism, or Christians back to earth, as in posttribulationism. Otherwise, they'd all stay suspended in midair forever and ever. So the mocking comment that at the second coming, posttribulationists have Christians going up and down like yo-yos doesn't wash. Besides, since a yo-yo goes down and up, not up and down, the comment is more apt for Jesus at a pretrib coming than for Christians at a posttrib coming.

Normally "descend," the word Paul uses in 1 Thessalonians 4:16–17, indicates a complete coming down, like that of the Holy Spirit at Jesus' baptism (Matt. 3:16; Mark 1:10; Luke 3:22; John 1:32, 33) and like that of Jesus' first advent (John 3:13; 6:33, 38, 41, 42, 50, 51, 58). A reversal from downward to upward motion prompts an explicit statement to that effect in Acts 10:11, 16 ("a certain object descending, . . . and immediately the object was taken up into heaven"). No statement of that sort appears in Paul's description of what happens at the rapture, or in any description of the second coming elsewhere in the New Testament.

Descending without Reversal

But since all indications point to the Lord's coming and gathering Christians after the tribulation and none to the same beforehand, why a catching up at all since he'll touch down soon enough anyway? "To meet the Lord in the air," Paul says. But why such a meeting? The answer is: to form a welcoming party that will escort the Lord on the last leg of his descent to earth. In the world of the New Testament it was common practice for a representative portion of citizenry to go out of their city a little distance, meet a visiting dignitary (say, the emperor, sometimes called "Lord"), and give him honor by escorting him on the last leg of his journey into the city. To provide a similarly fitting tribute to the Lord Jesus when he comes—that is the purpose of the

Meeting Christ to Escort Him the Rest of His Way Down

Abodes in Christ, Not Mansions in Heaven

rapture. It has nothing to do with exemption from the tribulation.

There's one more passage to discuss in this connection, John 14:2–3: "In my Father's household are many abodes. . . . I am going to prepare a place for you. And if I go and prepare a place for you, I am coming again; and I will receive you to myself in order that where I am, you may be also." "Household" or the more traditional translation "house"—it doesn't matter much for our purposes. The original Greek word can carry either meaning equally well, and often it's hard to distinguish between these meanings since a household lives in a house. More important is the word "abodes," for which the King James Version of the Bible has "mansions." But since the translation of the KJV nearly four hundred years ago, "mansion" has come to mean "any house of some size and pretension" (Webster). It used to mean an abode, pure and simple.

The original Greek word is the noun form of the verb "abide." Now this verb occurs numerous times in the context of John 14:2–3, that is, in the Upper Room Discourse of Jesus: "the Father abiding in me" (14:10); "he [the Spirit of truth] abides with you" (14:17); "abide in me and I in you . . . abides in the vine . . . abide in me" (15:4); "if any one does not abide in me, . . ." (15:6); "if you abide in me and my words abide in you, . . ." (15:7); "abide in my love" (15:9); "you will abide in my love . . . even as I have kept my Father's commandments and abide in his love" (15:10; see also John 6:56; 1 John 2:6, 10, 14, 24, 27, 28; 3:6, 9, 17, 24; 4:12, 13, 15, 16).

It's easy to see that the abodes which Jesus went to prepare for his disciples

aren't houses of some size and pretension
that he's building in heaven, as though he
were doing carpentry in the New Jerusalem. No, those abodes are abiding places
within himself ("Abide in me"), just as he
and his Father make their "abode" with the
person who loves Jesus and keeps his word
(John 14:23, the only other New Testament
passage besides verse 2 where the noun
"abode" occurs).

And where was Jesus going at the time he
spoke these words? To the cross. So what was
the nature of his preparation of those abiding
places in himself? His sacrificial death and resurrection. And when does he come again and
receive his disciples to himself in order that
they may be where he is? Well, if they abide in
him, they are where he is, and if they are abiding in him *now*, his coming again to receive
them must refer, not to a future coming, but to
his coming to the disciples immediately after
the resurrection to breathe on them and give
them the Spirit ("Jesus *came* . . . and breathed
on them and says to them, 'Receive the Holy
Spirit'"—John 20:19, 22; similarly verse 26:
"Jesus *comes* . . . and stood in the midst . . .";
compare 14:18: "I will not leave you orphaned,
I am *coming* to you"; 14:23 again: "we [my Father and I] will *come* and make an abode with
him [generic for anyone who loves Jesus and
keeps his word]"; 14:28: "I am *coming* to you"
[in connection with the Holy Spirit, given as
above at Jesus' coming in resurrection—note
the parallels between 14:25–27 and 20:19–23,
26]; and the whole of 16:16–24 concerning the
disciples' seeing Jesus again "in a little while").
In none of the other Gospels is the verb "come"
used for an appearance of the risen Jesus, as it
is in John's Gospel.

**Preparation as
Redemptive
Work, Not
Carpentry;
Coming in
Resurrection,
Not at the End**

Conclusion: John 14:2–3 isn't talking about the second coming and a rapture of Christians to heaven for the duration of the tribulation or of any other period of time, but about Jesus' coming to the disciples in resurrection after the crucifixion and providing them abodes in himself through giving them the Holy Spirit.

To Escort or Not to Escort

Note should be taken that the word for meeting, as in the expression "to meet the Lord in the air," doesn't *have* to indicate the meeting of a visiting dignitary to escort him on the last leg of his approach. But the capability of this word to carry that meaning gives a natural answer to the question, Why meet the Lord in the air only to turn around and come right back with him? For other meetings to return as an escort, see Matthew 25:1, 6; Acts 28:14b–16, not to list passages outside the New Testament; and for meetings not to return as an escort, see Mark 14:13; Luke 17:12 and some manuscripts of Matthew 27:32.

Taken or Left, Rapture or Judgment

In Matthew 24:40–41; Luke 17:34–35 the statement, "One is taken, one [or 'the other'] is left," may refer to being taken in rapture and left for judgment, or to being taken in judgment and left in safety. Since the context mentions both a judgment on the ungodly and a gathering of the elect, no very strong argument can be mounted on this statement for either pre- or posttribulationism.

Odds and End

9

The end—we'll take it up before the odds. Of course, "end" has many meanings, so we can't expect it always to carry the same meaning. In 1 Corinthians 15:24, for example, "the end" follows the coming of Christ (though by how much, it's debated). Elsewhere in contexts of the last things, however, the end and Christ's coming are wrapped in the same package: "What will be the sign of your coming and of the end of the age?" (Matt. 24:3); ". . . waiting for the revelation of our Lord Jesus Christ, who also will strengthen you till the end as blameless in the day of our Lord Jesus Christ" (1 Cor. 1:7–8); "But hold fast till I come; and the one who conquers and keeps my works to the end . . ." (Rev. 2:25–26; compare Matt. 10:22; 24:13; Mark 13:13 on disciples' enduring to the end).

Christ's Coming at the End

You'll have noticed that the coming of Christ with which the end is associated is his coming for which disciples are to watch and wait, and until which they are to do good works, be strengthened, and endure. That coming has to equate, therefore, with

The Rapture at the End

113

the coming at which the church's rapture occurs. Furthermore, the end is "of the age" (see Matt. 13:39, 40, 49; 28:20 as well as 24:3 again). This age has to be "the present evil age," as Paul describes it in Galatians 1:4, because watching and waiting and strengthening in good works won't be needed in the age to come. By then Jesus will have returned and rewarded his own. (For the distinction between this age and the coming one, see Matt. 12:32; Luke 20:34–35; Eph. 1:21, plus many other passages where one or the other is mentioned by itself.)

Nonarrival before the Trib

This end of the age toward which Christians are aiming—will it arrive before the tribulation? Jesus answers, No! The wars and rumors of wars and appearance of false Christs and earthquakes and famines—all the events that are commonly heralded as signs of the end, Jesus *denies* to be so: "But the end is not yet" (Mark 13:7). Such events characterize the normal course of history and therefore have no value for signaling the end:

> Beware that you not be led astray. For many will come in my name saying, . . . "The time is near." Do not go after them. And whenever you hear of wars and disturbances, do not be alarmed, for these things must happen first. But the end does not follow immediately (Luke 21:8–9; compare Matt. 24:14 on the end's not coming till the gospel has been preached throughout the world).

Signals of the End during the Trib

Jesus' tone changes when he comes to describe the tribulation, however. He portrays its events as distinctive and therefore

as signaling the end, marked by his coming
after the tribulation:

> But when you see the abomination of des-
> olation . . . , then the ones in Judea are to
> flee to the mountains. . . . For those days
> will be tribulation such as has not taken
> place since the beginning of the creation
> that God created till the present, and will
> not take place ever again. . . . When you
> see these things taking place, know that he
> [Jesus the Son of man] is near, at the doors
> (Mark 13:14–23, 28–31, excerpts; similarly
> Matt. 24:15–28, 32–35).

> And there will be signs in the sun and
> moon and stars, and on the earth distress
> among nations at a loss over the roaring of
> sea and waves, people fainting from fear
> and foreboding of what is coming on the
> world; for the powers of the heavens will
> be shaken . . . . Now as these things are be-
> ginning to happen, stand erect and lift up
> your heads, because your redemption is
> coming near (Luke 21:25–28).

> But immediately after the tribulation of
> those days, the sun will be darkened . . .
> and then will appear the sign of the Son of
> man in heaven, and then all the tribes of
> the earth will see the Son of man coming
> . . . (Matt. 24:29–30; similarly Mark 13:24–
> 27; Luke 21:27).

The End as Posttrib

So the end doesn't arrive with a coming
of Christ and rapture of the church before
the tribulation. It doesn't arrive even with
the tribulation, for the events of that period
only signal the end. The end arrives with
the coming of Christ *after* the tribulation,
and it's toward that end that Christians are

The Resurrection of Saints as Posttrib

to look and labor. The New Testament presents no other end as the lodestar of their activities.

Now that we've taken care of the end, let's take up the odds, that is, miscellaneous arguments that deserve at least a brief treatment. In describing the tribulation that precedes the end, Jesus borrowed phraseology from Daniel 12:1–2: "And there will be a time of tribulation such as has never been since nations came into existence . . . and at that time . . . many of those who sleep in the dust of the earth will awake, some to everlasting life and some to everlasting contempt." Here resurrection is associated with the tribulation, apparently as that which brings the tribulation to an end. Likewise, Jesus puts the resurrection—in particular, the resurrection of all that the Father has given him—"on the last day" (John 6:39, 40, 44, 54; 11:24). "The last day" sounds very like "the end," which follows the tribulation, as we have seen. So too does "the last trumpet," at which Paul puts the resurrection of deceased Christians and the translation of living ones (1 Cor. 15:51–52).

To "the last day," on which the resurrection occurs, we may also relate a contrast between the "day" (singular) of Jesus' coming after the tribulation and the preceding "days" (plural; see Matt. 24:19, 22, 29, 36–38, 42, 50; 25:13; Mark 13:17–32; Luke 17:22–31; 21:6, 22, 23, 34). And Revelation 20:4–6 puts "the first resurrection" of the "blessed and holy" after the tribulation in connection with Christ's coming and establishing his kingdom at that time (compare the resurrection and catching up of the two witnesses after "the holy city" and "the court outside the temple" have been "trampled by the nations for forty-two months," that is, after the second half of the tribulation—see Rev. 11:11–13 with verses 1–3 in the same chapter).

Consistently, then, the resurrection of saints is said to occur right after the tribulation. The New Testament mentions no other resurrection of saints. Paul distinguishes between their resurrection and that of Christ ("Christ the first fruits, then those who belong to Christ at his coming"—1 Cor. 15:23), but not between a pretrib resurrection of saints belonging to the church and a posttrib resurrection of another kind of saints.

Since the resurrection of saints is part and parcel of the second coming of Jesus and rapture of the church, the placement of that resurrection after the tribulation carries with it the placement of that coming and rapture after the tribulation. No surprise here, though. We've already seen that the Lord's descent, at which "the dead in Christ" will rise first and be caught up with living believers to meet him in the air—that descent coincides with the arrival of the Day of the Lord, which won't take place unless the Antichrist's rebellion and revelation come first (1 Thess. 4:13–5:11; 2 Thess. 2:1–5).

But doesn't the Holy Spirit have to be withdrawn from the earth before the Antichrist can do his thing during the tribulation? And since the Holy Spirit dwells in the church, won't the church have to be withdrawn along with the Holy Spirit? These are questions that people ask who've been

The Restraint and Restrainer of the Antichrist

taught pretribulationism. They're referring to 2 Thessalonians 2:6–8a.

The Uncertainty of a Reference to the Holy Spirit

To tell the truth, that passage doesn't even mention the Holy Spirit as a restraint or restrainer of the Antichrist. Neither does it say that the restrainer will be taken out of the world, only that he will get out of the way. Nor does the passage say that the restrainer uses the church as his instrument of restraint. Here's the passage: "And now you know what is restraining ['the man of lawlessness,' that is, the Antichrist], in order that he may be revealed in his own time. For the mystery of lawlessness is already working, only the one who is now restraining will do so until he gets out of the way."

Those who see the Holy Spirit in this passage note the shift from restraint to restrainer and appeal to the facts that in the Greek language, which Paul uses, the word "Spirit" is grammatically neuter (hence, "*what* is restraining") but theologically personal (hence, "the one *who* is now restraining"). But nowhere else does Paul use the neuter gender for the Holy Spirit unless he uses the Greek word for "Spirit." He doesn't use that word here, and there are other possibilities—for example, Roman law as a restraint against "the man of lawlessness," and the Roman emperor as the restrainer in enforcing that law; or divinely ordained human government and governmental officials in general; or Paul's evangelism as the restraint and he the evangelist as the restrainer—so that we're left guessing, and guessing doesn't provide a good argument for any view.

From Paul's oral teaching, the Thessalonians knew what and who he was writing about ("you know"). But we don't know. For the sake of argument, though, let's suppose that the restraint and restrainer are the Holy Spirit. Getting out of the way of the Antichrist's revelation doesn't have to entail exit from the world for both the Spirit and the church. The Spirit might be restraining the Antichrist apart from the church. In fact, it's hard to understand how the Spirit's dwelling in the church on earth keeps the Antichrist from appearing when it hasn't kept a lot of evil but less forceful figures from striding onto the stage of history. Where was the restraint when Hitler came along? Stalin? Mao Zedong? The church was still here!

Doubt concerning the Church's Instrumentality

Furthermore, as all sides agree, there'll be saints of one kind or another—and an innumerable company of them at that—on earth during the tribulation when the Antichrist is revealed and leads his rebellion against all divinity but his own falsely alleged divinity. Why wouldn't the presence of these saints on earth restrain the Antichrist as much as that of the church is supposed to? Or are we really supposed to think that after a pretrib rapture of the church, worldwide evangelism and innumerable conversions will take place despite an absence of the Holy Spirit, or despite a significant reduction of the Spirit's presence, as in the Old Testament period, so much of a reduction that the presence on earth of saints not belonging to the church won't restrain the Antichrist? Come now—less Holy Spirit, less evangelistic success.

Again, the Undeniable Presence of Saints on Earth during the Tribulation

Out of the Way, Not Necessarily out of the World

All that 2 Thessalonians 2:6–8a requires is that someone is restraining the Antichrist. The restraint may be applied directly, apart from the church rather than indirectly through the church. And the restrainer's getting out of the way doesn't have to mean leaving the world, only getting out of the way of the Antichrist's revelation. More than that is sheer supposition, not good argument. And let's remind ourselves that this passage is sandwiched between references to Christians' being relieved from persecution at Jesus' coming to judge their persecutors, to his coming and our being gathered to him on the Day of the Lord that won't arrive till after the Antichrist's rebellion and revelation, and to the Lord's coming to destroy the Antichrist—all posttribulational (see 1:4–2:5, 8).

Sorrow and Disturbance

But if all posttribulational, some pretrib teachers ask why the Thessalonian Christians weren't sorrowing over themselves rather than over their deceased fellow Christians, for at least their deceased fellow Christians didn't have to face the possibility of going through the tribulation whereas they the living did have to face that possibility (1 Thess. 4:13). Teachers of pretribulationism also ask why the Thessalonian Christians were "shaken" and "disturbed" because of their false belief that the Day of the Lord had already arrived, unless Paul had taught them that day includes the tribulation and begins with or comes after the rapture, so that they thought of the day's presence as implying they had missed the rapture (2 Thess. 2:1–2).

The first question, the one about sorrowing, overlooks that Paul commended the Thessalonian Christians for "having received the word in much tribulation with the joy of the Holy Spirit" (1:6; compare Acts 17:1–13). They had considered it "a privilege not only to believe in Christ but also to suffer for him" (Phil. 1:29). And in part, this first question also overlooks that the Thessalonian Christians did become disturbed over their own prospects, as indicated in the second question, the one about being shaken and disturbed.

The Privilege of Suffering for Christ

In reference to the second question, which deals with the Thessalonian Christians' self-concern, they were in communication with Paul, Silvanus, and Timothy (1 Thess. 1:1; 2 Thess. 1:1). So if they were disturbed through thinking they had missed a pretrib rapture, they must have also thought that even the apostle and his helpers had missed it—an unlikely thought, not only in itself but also in view of Paul's not making an argument out of the facts that he and his helpers were still around and that "the churches of God" were, too (2 Thess. 1:4).

The Unlikelihood of Thinking of a Missed Rapture

What Paul does argue is that the Day of the Lord can't come until the "rebellion comes first and the man of lawlessness is revealed" (2 Thess. 2:3). Much more likely, then, the Thessalonian Christians made the mistakes of thinking the Day of the Lord will include the tribulation and of thinking they had entered the first part of that day, so they got shook up at the thought that they were about to suffer increasingly worse persecution than they had suffered before. It's one thing to take persecution

The Likelihood of Thinking the Day of the Lord Had Already Started with the Trib

with the joy of the Holy Spirit and a sense of privilege at the time you're undergoing the persecution. It's another thing, and quite natural, to dread persecution ahead of time, especially when you think it's going to be worse than ever and is on the very verge of striking. This is the reported experience of Christians who've suffered persecution in our own times.

The Likelihood of Disbelief in a Future Resurrection

Other teachers of pretribulationism take quite a different tack and ask why the Thessalonian Christians were sorrowing if it wasn't because they thought that their deceased fellow Christians were going to miss a pretrib rapture and not be raised till after the tribulation. But they could just as easily have thought that the deceased were going to miss a posttrib rapture and not be raised till after an earthly rule of Christ. It's better, though, to think that the sorrow grew out of a lack of belief in the resurrection of deceased believers at *any* future moment. Paul's wanting the Thessalonians not to sorrow "as also the others [unbelievers] who have no hope" greatly favors this view, which gets further though indirect support from the nearby Corinthian Christians' disbelief in a future resurrection of deceased fellow Christians even though they did believe in Christ's past resurrection (1 Cor. 15:1–58).

Along with resurrection go judgment and reward, as in the distinction between "the resurrection of life" and "the resurrection of judgment" (John 5:29). In another sense, however, we'll all be judged, though we'll not all be condemned: "For we must all appear before the judgment seat of Christ in order that each person may get repaid for the things done through the body, whether good or evil" (2 Cor. 5:10).

Now teachers of pretribulationism usually distinguish the judgment seat of Christ from the judgment of "all the nations" in Matthew 25:31–46 as well as from other judgments, such as "the great white throne" judgment described in Revelation 20:11–15. According to these distinctions, the judgment seat of Christ has to do with Christians and their eternal rewards, and takes place in heaven during the tribulation. The judgment of all the nations takes place on earth at Jesus' return after the tribulation and has to do with people still living on earth at that time and with their admission or nonadmission into Jesus' earthly kingdom, called "the millennium" or "thousand years" in Revelation 20:4–6. And the great white throne judgment takes place between that millennial kingdom and the eternal state, in the void between the old and new heavens and earth, and has to do with the unsaved who have died throughout human history and with their eternal punishment.

Pretrib Distinctions between Judgments

Whatever their validity or invalidity, these distinctions between judgments do not make an argument against Christ's coming back only after the tribulation. Someone who believes only in a posttrib coming could hold the distinctions and simply shift the time and place of the judgment seat of Christ from heaven and the tribulation to earth and the coming of Christ after the tribulation. But the distinctions themselves are questionable in the extreme. Nothing in 2 Corinthians 5:10 locates the judgment seat of Christ spatially

The Indecisiveness and Doubtfulness of Distinctions between Judgments

in heaven or chronologically in the tribulation. And though Paul was writing to Christians and probably had them in mind most of all, it is at least arguable that his addition of "all" to "we," his follow-up with "each person," and his mention of "evil" as well as "good" are meant to bring in everybody, not just Christians. Even an exclusive *reference* to Christians wouldn't have to exclude non-Christians from the judgment, for Paul could simply be singling out the one group because he was addressing them directly.

Nothing in Matthew 25:31–46 indicates that the judgment of all the nations has to do with admission or nonadmission into Jesus' *millennial* kingdom. On the contrary, some will go "into eternal punishment" and "the righteous into eternal life" (verse 46), so that "inherit the kingdom prepared for you from the foundation of the world" (verse 34) refers more easily to the eternal state than to a millennial state. And if the great white throne judgment has to do only with unsaved people, what are we to make of the "if" in Revelation 20:15: "And *if* anyone was not found written in the book of life"? It seems to imply the presence of saved people who *are* written in that book.

A General Judgment

To make a distinction between "the judgment seat of Christ" and "the great white throne" merely on the basis of different wording is as mistaken as making distinctions among "the Day of the Lord," "the Day of Christ," "the Day of Christ Jesus," "the Day of our Lord Jesus," and "the Day of our Lord Jesus Christ" on the same basis. You might as well distinguish between "the judgment seat of Christ" in 2 Corinthians 5:10 and "the judgment seat of God" in Romans 14:10 (according to the earliest and best manuscripts)—yet Paul is writing to Christians in both passages. It's truer to the Bible to think of a general judgment, saved and unsaved all present, at the juncture between history and eternity.

The following question is a pretrib attempt to turn the tables: If posttribulationism is true, why doesn't Paul say in 2 Thessalonians 2:1–5 that we can tell the Day of the Lord hasn't arrived because a *post*tribulational rapture hasn't yet occurred prior to the Day of the Lord? The answer is simple: the likely mistakes of Thessalonian Christians were to think of the Day of the Lord as including the tribulation and to think of themselves as having entered the first part of that day or tribulation, so Paul couldn't assume their accepting that the posttrib rapture will occur before the Day of the Lord. Besides, other events haven't yet occurred that must happen earlier than the posttrib rapture. The citation of even earlier events— that is, the rebellion and the Antichrist's revelation—lends greater force to Paul's denial that the Day of the Lord has arrived. New Year's Day doesn't come till after Christmas, but if not even Thanksgiving has yet arrived, it packs more punch to say it's still before Thanksgiving than to say it's still before Christmas.

Reasons Why Paul Didn't Cite the Nonoccurrence of a Posttrib Rapture

Elsewhere in the New Testament, "out of the way"—the phrase used by Paul in 2 Thessalonians 2:7 for the restrainer's withdrawing himself from between the Anti-

Withdrawal without Exit

christ and that one's revelation—occurs for withdrawal from the world only in Matthew 13:49. In all the remaining passages, six of them, it occurs for a withdrawal *without* exit from the world (see Acts 17:33; 23:10; 1 Cor. 5:2; 2 Cor. 6:17; Col. 2:14—English translations varying according to differences of subject matter in the context). Since the present fulness of the Holy Spirit grows out of the resurrection and exaltation of Jesus as Lord and Christ (see Acts 2:14–36, especially verses 32–33), those who would see a reduction of the Spirit's presence and power during the tribulation—that is, a return to the Old Testament state of affairs—have some tall explaining to do.

The Simultaneity of First Resurrection and Second Coming

The argument has been made that "the first resurrection" in Revelation 20:4–6 follows the second coming in Revelation 19:11–16 and therefore can't equate with the resurrection that occurs right *at* the second coming in connection with the church's rapture (1 Thess. 4:16–17). But in Revelation 19:11–20:6 John is simply ticking off things that happen in one and the same episode of the Second Coming, not stringing them out always in chronological succession.

For example, the statement in 19:19, "And I saw the Beast and the kings of the earth and their armies gathered to make war with the one sitting on the horse [Jesus Christ] and with his army," follows the statement in 19:11, "And I saw heaven opened and, behold, a white horse and the one sitting on it called 'Faithful and True.' . . . And the armies in heaven were following him. . . . " Yet the gathering of the Beast and kings and earthly armies cannot follow the second coming, because another passage has already put the gathering earlier, in the sixth bowl, not the seventh (16:12–16). Furthermore, right within Revelation 20:4–6 John mentions the saints' sitting on thrones to rule before he mentions that the saints have risen from the dead, though obviously they have to rise before they can rule. So we shouldn't conclude that the first resurrection takes place later than the second coming from the mere fact that the first resurrection isn't mentioned till after the second coming as such has been described.

It is often argued that if the church is raptured at Jesus' return after the tribulation and all non-Christians living at that time are judged, nobody will be left to populate the earth during the millennial kingdom. But will all non-Christians living at the time be judged in the sense of barred from that kingdom? Only if you assume either that the second coming entails the death of all non-Christians or that Matthew 25:31–46 deals with admission or nonadmission into the millennial kingdom. On the contrary, we've noted above that that passage deals with the alternatives of "eternal punishment" and "eternal life."

Populating the Millennial Earth

Teachers of pretribulationism usually interpret Jesus' "brothers" in the passage as the Jewish people, so that admission or nonadmission of Gentiles into the millennial kingdom depends on their treatment of Jews. But earlier, in Matthew 12:50, Jesus identified the disciples ("whoever does the will of my Father in heaven") as his "brother and sister and mother." Still earlier, in Matthew 10:40–42, he said that the

Jesus' Brothers as Disciples, Not Jews

person receiving them received him, and that giving "one of these little ones" even a drink of cold water would bring a reward. This language sounds remarkably close to that in the judgment of all the nations, where doing an act of charity to "one of these littlest brothers of mine" equates with doing it to Jesus himself. The judgment doesn't have to do with Gentiles' treatment of Jews, then, but with Christians' proving the genuineness of their profession by exposing themselves to danger in providing shelter, food, drink, and clothing to fellow Christians who are fleeing persecution (compare Matt. 10:23: "But when they persecute you in this city, flee into the next") and in visiting fellow Christians who've been caught and imprisoned.

The Entrance of Unsaved People into the Millennium

Though Ezekiel 20:32–38 is often cited to prove that only saved Jews will enter the millennial kingdom, that passage deals with the restoration of a Jewish remnant to their land following the Babylonian exile long ago. And though texts that talk of universal judgment aren't hard to come by (take 2 Thess. 1:6–10; 2:9–12, for instance), it would be hard to prove that the second coming entails the death and immediate banishment to hell of all unsaved people on earth. That some of them both survive and enter the millennial kingdom seems clear enough from Zechariah 14:16: ". . . everyone who is left of all the nations that came against Jerusalem will go up from year to year to worship the King, the LORD of Hosts." These can't consist of people born during the millennial kingdom, because Zechariah describes them as "everyone who is *left* of all the nations that came against Jerusalem." Nor can they consist of people saved during the tribulation, because Zechariah goes on to hold out the possibility that some of them will "*not* go up to Jerusalem to worship the king, the LORD of hosts" and will therefore receive "the punishment" of a "plague" (14:17–19).

It's amazing that teachers of pretribulationism who argue from a supposed problem of populating the millennial earth commonly pass over Zechariah 14:16–19 in silence, and that the occasional one who does pay some attention to it still manages to overlook the implications of "left" and "not." And if not to overlook those implications, to suppose that only later, unregenerate offspring of the saved people who enter the millennium will refuse to make pilgrimage to Jerusalem—this postponement of such a refusal allows saved people alone to enter the millennium; but it also wrenches verses 17–19 from the context provided by verse 16, and the purely suppositional nature of such a postponement exposes weakness in the pretrib argument.

If unsaved survivors of the tribulation enter the millennium, of course, the destruction of wicked armies gathered at Armageddon doesn't match the universal scope of the saints' rapture, which occurs on the same occasion. But nothing in the scriptural text forbids this asymmetry, which therefore doesn't argue against posttribulationism. And right within *pre*tribulationism there's a similar asymmetry between a resurrection and reward restricted to millennial saints at the close of the millennium, and at the same time a resurrection and judgment including all the wicked before the great white throne.

A Case of Mistaken Identity

In this regard Hal Lindsey, the most successful recent popularizer of pretribulationalism, wrote that in "a short debate" which he had with me "before the student body at Westmont College," he "hit" me "with the question of who will populate the Kingdom," and I "had no answer for it."[1] The truth is that I've never seen Lindsey in the flesh, only on the tube. The college chaplain, a friend of his and mine, asked me to take part in the debate, but another commitment prevented me both from doing so and from attending. It was later reported to me that Lindsey debated a local pastor—over the issue of whether Christ will return before the millennium, not over the issue of whether he'll return before the tribulation. The prophetic question of who will populate the millennial kingdom thus gives way to the historical question of who populated the debate, and what the debate was about.

Fair and Square

As to the pretrib argument that it wouldn't be fair of God to give the wicked who survive the tribulation and second coming a chance to be saved during the millennium after they didn't take their earlier chance for salvation—well, what about the fairness of God according to *pre*tribulationism? He gives the wicked a chance to be saved after the rapture though they didn't take their earlier chance for salvation. As mentioned before, pretrib teachers are even marketing a videotape to be used after the

1. Hal Lindsey, *The Rapture: Truth or Consequences* (New York: Bantam Books, 1983) 148–49.

rapture for the evangelism of these people. And there are all sorts of apparent injustices in the varying opportunities and influences that bear on people's salvation. What about those who rejected Christ during his earthly ministry but were given another chance after his resurrection, for example? None of us are equipped to answer such questions. We'll have to wait for God to answer them at the last judgment. Meanwhile, whether or not anybody thinks it fair, the biblical text indicates that wicked people will enter the millennial kingdom.

That a general judgment of all the nations can include Jews as well as Gentiles and come after the millennium even though mentioned in association with the second coming beforehand—these possibilities are demonstrated by a comprehensive use of "all the nations" in the Great Commission (Matt. 28:19–20; compare 24:9, 14; Rom. 16:26; Rev. 14:8; 18:3), by "every nation" in Revelation 5:9; 14:6, by "many nations" in Revelation 10:11, and by passages where "nations" includes Jews as well as Gentiles even without "all," "every," or "many" (see, for example, Rom. 4:17, 18; Rev. 21:24). These possibilities are also demonstrated by the association of judgment for the dead, wicked as well as righteous, with Jesus' coming after the tribulation (Rev. 11:18; compare 22:12) even though the very same book says that the wicked dead are raised for judgment not till after the millennium (see Rev. 20:11–15 with verses 1–10). **Ethnic Universality of Judgment**

A general judgment taking place after the millennium would cover the whole of human history, of course, not just the millennium. So utopian conditions in the mil- **Temporal Universality of Judgment** lennium wouldn't rule out bringing up at the judgment earlier conditions of homelessness, hunger, thirst, nakedness, and imprisonment in accordance with Matthew 25:31–46. In pretribulationism, too, the judgment that takes place at "the great white throne" covers the whole of human history for the wicked, and therefore nonutopian conditions, though the millennium has immediately preceded.

The Nations as Alive by Resurrection   The further pretrib argument that since "nations" usually refers to the living rather than to the dead, the judgment of "all the nations" in Matthew 25:31–46 must differ from the judgment of "the dead" in Revelation 20:11–15—this argument overlooks that these dead are "the rest of the dead" who have "come to life" in the second resurrection, following the millennium, for the purpose of "standing" before the great white throne (Rev. 20:5, 12; compare 21:24, 26; 22:2 for other postresurrectional uses of "nations," and 5:6 for "standing" as an indication that resurrection of the dead has taken place: the "slain Lamb" is "standing"). And the yet further pretrib argument that the judgment of all nations takes place on earth whereas judgment at the great white throne takes place after the earth has "fled away" along with the heaven—this argument reads an earthly locale into Matthew's text. You'll find there no reference to the earth at all.

A Short Discussion of Long Odds on Other Distinctions That Make No Difference

10

A distinction between judgments is one thing, but teachers of pretribulationism display a fondness for making other distinctions, too, and neglect the facts that all writers, biblical ones included, often use different terminology for the same subject matter even within their own writings, much more by comparison with each other's writings, and that they don't mention all aspects of the second coming or of any other topic every time they bring it up. A resurrection isn't mentioned every time the second coming is brought up, for example, yet everybody agrees that one occurs in connection with that event (*wherever* the event is put on the time-line). Paul mentions a coming, a resurrection of the dead, and a rapture but

Variety of Expression and Emphasis

no translation of living saints in 1 Thessalonians 4:16–17, a coming and a gathering (that is, rapture) but no resurrection or translation in 2 Thessalonians 2:1, a resurrection and a translation but no coming or rapture in 1 Corinthians 15:51–52. Yet teachers of pretribulationism correctly see all three passages as describing various elements in one and the same overall event.

Examples of this sort could be multiplied indefinitely. So falls flat the making of distinctions not only between judgments but also between pre- and posttrib comings of Christ on the bases of differing terminology ("Son of man," "Lord," "Christ," "coming," "blessed hope," "glorious appearing," "revelation," etc.) and of mention or omission of this or that associated element (signs, a shout, an archangel, a trumpet, a resurrection, a translation, an upward rapture, "the air," Armageddon, judgment, reward, etc.). Variety is the spice of life—and of biblical writings, too.

The Jewishness of Daniel's Seventieth Week

Daniel 9:24–27 contains a prophecy of seventy weeks concerning the nation of Israel. Each week consists of seven years, not of seven days. Those who believe in a future tribulation, as both pre- and posttribulationists do, generally regard it as equivalent to Daniel's seventieth week. Therefore teachers of pretribulationism sometimes argue that since God wasn't dealing with the church during the first sixty-nine weeks, he won't be dealing with the church during the seventieth week, either.

The Gentileness of Daniel's Seventieth Week

But of course the church didn't yet exist during the first sixty-nine weeks, and the New Testament often applies to the church Old Testament passages having to do with Israel (a striking example: God's once again calling rejected Israel his people applies also to God's calling Christian Gentiles his people even though they've never been such before—Rom. 9:25–26, quoting Hos. 1:10 and 2:23 in reverse order). In pretribulationism itself, God will deal savingly during the seventieth week with an innumerable throng of Gentiles wholly unmentioned in Daniel 9:24–27 or in any other Old Testament passage (see Rev. 7:9–17). So progress in the biblical history of salvation makes the situation in a future seventieth week different from what it was during the past sixty-nine weeks. You can't legitimately argue from one to the other.

Teachers of pretribulationism also argue as follows: The translation of living saints that accompanies the resurrection of deceased ones, both of them in preparation for the rapture—that translation is called "a mystery" in 1 Corinthians 15:51–52. A mystery consists of a truth revealed for the first time in the New Testament. But Daniel's seventieth week, the tribulation, was revealed already in the Old Testament. So the mystery concerning a translation of living saints that's tied up with the rapture can't happen in connection with the seventieth week, or tribulation. Otherwise it wouldn't be a mystery.

The Mystery of Translation

This line of argument suffers from several fatal flaws. First, for the argument to work at all, the translation of living saints would have to occur while the tribulation, or seventieth week, was still going on, even though at its very last moment. But in posttribulationism the translation that's tied up with the rapture or gathering of the saints doesn't occur till *"after* the tribulation," as

The Translation as Post-Seventieth Week

Jesus himself said (Matt. 24:29–31; Mark 13:24–27).

Mystery in the Seventieth Week

Second, though a translation were to take place at the very last moment of the tribulation, or Daniel's seventieth week, the translation as such could still be called a mystery without pushing it to a pretribulational position. For there's nothing to keep the New Testament from adding mysteries to a period of time already revealed in the Old Testament.

Third, Paul makes just such an addition, in fact. It's "the mystery of lawlessness," which, as pretribulationists agree, reaches its climax during the seventieth week, or tribulation, in the career of the man of lawlessness, the Antichrist, though that mystery "is already at work" (2 Thess. 2:7–12; see also Rev. 10:7 for "the mystery of God" that "comes to completion" during the tribulation, specifically "in the days of the sound of the seventh trumpet"). So the translation's being a mystery doesn't put it outside the tribulation even though it *is* outside the tribulation—only afterward, not beforehand.

Mosaic Law in the Seventieth Week: Nonbinding

Jewish observance of the Mosaic law needn't be a divine requirement during the tribulation any more than it is now. Thus, for example, Jesus' commanding the disciples in Judea to pray that their flight during the tribulation not occur on a Sabbath doesn't imply that they ought to keep the Sabbath (Matt. 24:20). Sabbath or no, they are to flee (Matt. 24:16; Mark 13:14). Praying that the flight not occur on the Sabbath implies only that the resting of other Jews on the Sabbath would make the flight of Christians obvious, difficult, and dangerous, just as in the very same verse praying that the flight not occur during winter implies storms that would make flight obvious, difficult, and dangerous.

Likewise, the "gospel of the kingdom" to be preached "in the whole of the inhabited earth" (Matt. 24:14) isn't a gospel tailored for the tribulation and differing from the gospel preached now. The parallel passage has "the gospel" without qualification (Mark 13:10), and Paul was preaching "the kingdom of God" well into the church age (Acts 28:30–31; compare Rom. 14:17; 1 Cor. 4:20; Col. 1:13; 4:11).

The Gospel of the Kingdom in the Seventieth Week: Non-Jewish

Though it doesn't cut very much ice with nontheologians, the biggest distinction made in pretribulationism has to do with Israel and the church. Here's the way it goes. The church has replaced Israel for the time being. Therefore the church differs from Israel. God doesn't deal with the church and Israel at the same time; there's a clean break, no overlap, between his dealings with them. During the tribulation he will be dealing with Israel. Therefore the church will have to be absent; and for her to be absent, Christ will have to return before the tribulation to take her out of the world.

Pretrib Insistence on a Clean Break

This chain of reasoning disregards the lack of scriptural support for a return of Christ and rapture just before the tribulation. Worse yet, it disregards scriptural indications that those events won't occur till after the tribulation. Within the chain of reasoning itself, the weakest link consists in supposing that God doesn't deal with the church and Israel at the same time, so that there's a clean break between "dispensations." Scripturally, that supposition is false.

Posttrib Evidence for an Overlap

According to Matthew 11:13 and Luke 16:16, the prophets and the law ceased with John the Baptist, not later on the Day of Pentecost (the so-called "birthday of the church"). The new cloth and new wine of the new dispensation are reflected in the behavior of Jesus' disciples some time before his ascension and bestowal of the Holy Spirit at Pentecost (Matt. 9:14–17; Luke 5:33–39). Jesus abrogated Jewish dietary laws while still ministering to Jews (Mark 7:18–19; note how this abrogation is recorded for the sake and from the standpoint of Gentiles in the church age—verses 3–4). "The law was given through Moses; grace and truth came through Jesus Christ" (John 1:17), so that the age of the church, free from the Mosaic Law, did not start cleanly and without antecedent on the Day of Pentecost (Acts 2:1–47), but had roots reaching back into the period of Jesus' ministry to Israel. Even on and after the Day of Pentecost, the gospel went first to the Jews for their national restoration (Acts 2:39 and especially 3:12–26), and the gift of the Holy Spirit came tardily to Samaritan believers (Acts 8:9–24).

God had his Son Jesus forming the nucleus of the church by choosing the twelve apostles and making other early disciples—except for Judas Iscariot, they were the ones on whom the Holy Spirit descended at Pentecost (Acts 1:12–2:4)—at the same time he had his Son Jesus trying to reform Israel (compare especially Matt. 16:18; Mark 3:14; Luke 6:13 with Matt. 10:5–6; 11:1; 15:24; 23:37; Luke 13:33–34). And long after the church age had come into full bloom, God was dealing also with Israel at the destruction of Jerusalem and the temple in A.D. 70 (compare Matt. 24:1–2; Mark 13:1–2; Luke 21:5–6, 20–24).

Taking for granted that God will deal with Israel during the tribulation, we can equally well suppose he'll deal also with the church around the time of the second coming just as he dealt simultaneously with both Israel and the church around the time of the first coming. If the pretrib argument is refined to say that God doesn't deal with two different entities *of salvation* at the same time, it's enough to reply that during the tribulation the church will remain the sole entity of salvation just as she was when he was dealing also with Israel at the destruction of Jerusalem and the temple in A.D. 70.

Simultaneous Dealings

Valid though it is, moreover, the distinction between Israel and the church has been overplayed in pretribulationism. Among other scriptural indications of a fundamental unity binding these two entities together, note the grafting of Gentile believers into the stock of Israel according to Romans 11:17–24, the statement in Hebrews 11:40 that apart from New Testament believers the Old Testament heroes of faith won't be brought to completion, and the inscriptions of the names of the twelve Israelite tribes and of the twelve apostles of the church on the gates and foundations, respectively, of the New Jerusalem (Rev. 21:12, 14). Right within the dispensational school of thought associated with pretribulationism, so-called "progressive dispensationalists" are recognizing this unity. So the

The Underlying Unity of Israel and the Church

biggest distinction of all—the one between Israel and the church—fails to support pretribulationism.

Pretrib Misreadings of the Biblical Text: Air and Earth

Teachers of pretribulationism often display so much desire to see unharmonizable distinctions between two separate stages of the second coming that they misread the biblical text. For example, they say that before the tribulation Jesus comes "in the air," after the tribulation "to the earth." But 1 Thessalonians 4:17 speaks of Christians' "meeting" him in the air, not of his "coming" in the air; and there's nothing in the passage to indicate that he can't come on down to the earth after Christians have met him in the air. And though all sides agree that at one time or another he does come down to the earth, as such the phrase "to the earth" never appears in the New Testament for the second coming, so that the setting up of a contrast between "in the air" and "to the earth" not only misreads the first phrase. It also invents the second one.

Secrecy and Publicity

Another example of misreading: Jesus' pretrib coming will be secret, "as a thief," whereas "every eye will see him" at his coming after the tribulation. But "as a thief" has to do with unexpectedness, not with secrecy: "when they are saying, 'Peace and safety'" (1 Thess. 5:2–3); "at an hour that you think not" (Matt. 24:42–44); "you will not know at what hour I will come upon you" (Rev. 3:3)—all in connection with the figure of a thief's coming. Not to mention what we've already noted, that the contexts of Matthew 24:42–44 and Revelation 16:15

link Jesus' coming as a thief with his coming "after the tribulation."

A final example of misreading is found in the contrast often made between a pretrib coming as joyful and blessed and the posttrib coming as mournful and judgmental. To take but two texts by way of refutation: 2 Thessalonians 1:3–10 puts the "relief" of Christians from their persecution at the very same coming of Christ at which the wicked are judged "with flaming fire." And in Revelation 19:1–21 the coming of Christ excites a fourfold "Hallelujah!" on the very occasion of his "striking the nations with the sword of his mouth." What's blessed for some is judgmental for others. No need here to separate different comings of Jesus from each other.

Joy and Mourning

PERSPECTIVE 11

Most people who've been taught pretribulationism all their lives, or at least since their conversion to Christ, assume that it's pretty much what true Christians have believed about the second coming down through the centuries. You can easily understand the assumption. Usually, no other point of view has been presented to these people. They may not even know there's another. And if they have been made aware, any view other than pretribulationism has almost certainly been presented as unbiblical, if not heretical, and has probably been presented only in passing, without seriously engaging and possibly without so much as mentioning any scriptural arguments for another view and against pretribulationism.

A Wrong Assumption

As a matter of fact, pretribulationism is the new kid on the block when it comes to what Christians have believed the New Testament teaches about Jesus' return in relation to the tribulation and the Antichrist. We're dealing here with perspective, of course, not with proof. For Bible-believing

The Novelty of Pretribulationism

Christians, proof lies in the pages of Scripture, and the view that seems to represent its meaning most naturally is the view that seems best to adopt. Agreed. But Christians belong not only to current communities of faith. They also belong to a community of faith that spans the whole of church history. And since the Spirit of God has been at work throughout that history, Christians should at least respect primary beliefs of the church at large, past as well as present, and suspect the new and novel at least to the extent of requiring extraordinarily good scriptural evidence in its favor. This kind of historical perspective can keep Christians from flying off into the weird and wild, bizarre and outlandish.

The Antiquity of Posttribulationism

From earliest centuries onward, the standard Christian view was that the church would enter the tribulation, confront the Antichrist, and come out not till Jesus' return following the tribulation. During the earliest centuries every writer who touched in any detail on the second coming represented this view, which nowadays we call posttribulationism. Its opposite number, pretribulationism, didn't become widely held in any Christian circles till the mid- or late 1800s and early 1900s.

The Precarious Beginning of Pretribulationism

The point is somewhat disputed, but so far as has been discovered in known literature, pretribulationism probably wasn't even thought up by anyone until the late 1700s or early 1800s. And when it was, it didn't look like contemporary pretribulationism. It didn't have a full seven years separating Christ's coming for the church from his coming with the church. It may not even have had all the church raptured before the tribulation. And it certainly didn't capture the allegiance of most Christians throughout the main branches of Christendom.

But let's start early and put our emphasis there, because Christians living then established the New Testament canon, formulated the historic creeds of the church, and inherited their beliefs straight from the apostles themselves. Not that those Christians couldn't and didn't make mistakes, and also disagree with each other. They did on some matters. But on the second coming, tribulation, and Antichrist, their writings present a view about as strong and uniform as could be imagined. Here's the evidence:

Early Posttribulationism

As noted a number of times earlier, the saying of Jesus recorded in Matthew 24:30–31 and its parallel Mark 13:26–27 puts the gathering of the elect at his coming right after the tribulation. Well, late in the first century already, or early in the second, *The Teaching of the Twelve Apostles* quoted that saying twice and substituted "the church" for "the elect" (9:4; 10:5). This document went on to tell Christians that they must stand firm through the reign of the Antichrist, which as in other early Christian literature is set out in the future, right up to Jesus' subsequent coming and the accompanying resurrection of the saints:

The Teaching of the Twelve Apostles

> Watch out for your life. Do not let your lamps be put out or your waists unbelted. But be ready, for you do not know the hour in which our Lord is coming. [Here several pretrib writers misleadingly break off the quotation to make the passage look

as though it teaches that Christ may return at any moment and therefore before the tribulation] . . . for the whole time of your faith will not profit you unless you have reached the goal at the last time. . . . And then the world-deceiver [that is, the Antichrist] will appear as though [he is] God's Son and will perform signs and wonders. . . . Then the creation consisting of human beings will come into the fire of trial, and many will be caused to stumble and will perish. But the ones who endure in their faith will be saved . . . (16:1–8).

The Epistle of Barnabas

Again in the late first or early second century, *The Epistle of Barnabas* encouraged Christians to stand firm both in the present evil time and in the coming tribulation:

The final stumbling-block is near . . . [here the author launches into a discussion of the Beast, or Antichrist]. Therefore we are to pay attention in the last days; for the whole [past] time of our faith will profit us nothing unless now in this lawless time we resist also the coming stumbling blocks . . . in order that the Black One [Antichrist] may not have a way of slipping in (4:3–9).

The Shepherd of Hermas

In the second century, *The Shepherd of Hermas* pronounced the beatitude, "Blessed are you, as many as endure the great tribulation that is coming and as many as will not deny their life . . . their Christ" (*Vision* 2.2.7), and wrote further,

Go therefore and relate to the elect of the Lord his great deeds, and tell them that this beast is a type of the great tribulation that is going to come. If then you prepare yourselves ahead of time and repent with your whole heart toward the Lord, it will be possible for you to escape it.

Escape? Sounds like a pretrib rapture, doesn't it? Not if you read on:

> Believe the Lord, you double-minded ones, that he can do all things and is turning his anger away from you and sending scourges on you the double-minded ones. . . . Those therefore who remain and pass through the flames will be purified by them. . . . You have also the type of the great tribulation that is coming. But if you want, it will be nothing (*Vision* 4.2.5–6; 4.3.4, 6).

In other words, be a genuine Christian and you won't suffer God's wrath but you'll be purified by what else you do suffer. Escape at the far end of the tribulation, not by prior removal.

Justin Martyr

Still in the second century, the early church leader Justin Martyr equated the hope of Christians with Jesus' return to the earth, as prophesied in the Old Testament, not with a partial return into the air as supposedly revealed in the New Testament, and Justin placed the resurrection and gathering of Christians at the beginning of the millennium, not before the preceding tribulation (*Dialogue with Trypho* 52, 80–81). Yet more clearly, he also wrote that "the man of apostasy [Antichrist] . . . will venture to do unlawful deeds on the earth against us the Christians . . ." (*Dialogue with Trypho* 110).

Irenaeus

Late in the second century the early church leader Irenaeus, who had been taught by Polycarp who in turn had been taught by the Apostle John, wrote, "And they [the ten kings represented by the ten horns of the Beast in Rev. 17:12] will . . . give their kingdom to the Beast and put the church to flight" (*Against Heresies* 5.26.1). Again, "But he [John] indicates the number of the name now [666 for the Beast, or Antichrist—Rev. 13:18] in order that when this man comes we may avoid him by being aware who he is" (*Against Heresies* 5.30.4). Irenaeus also put the resurrection of the church after the Antichrist's rule rather than beforehand (*Against Heresies* 5.34.3; 5.35.1).

Gallic Churches   The churches of Vienna and Lugdunum in Gaul (modern-day France) wrote a letter to the churches in Asia and Phrygia (Roman provinces in modern-day Turkey). The letter describes a recent persecution as something like the persecution that Satan will incite against the whole church during the tribulation: "For with all his strength the adversary attacked us, even then giving a foretaste of his activity among us which is going to be without restraint. . . ."

Tertullian   During the late second and early third centuries the North African church leader Tertullian linked the rapture of the church as described in 1 Thessalonians 4:16–17 with Christ's coming to destroy the Antichrist and set up his own kingdom on earth after the tribulation. Likewise, he linked the resurrection of the "church" with that coming (*Against Marcion* 3.25; *On the Resurrection of the Flesh* 24) and went on to write,

> . . . that the Beast Antichrist with his false prophet may wage war on the church of

God. . . . Since then the Scriptures both indicate the stages of the last time and concentrate the harvest of the Christian hope in the very end of the world . . . (*On the Resurrection of the Flesh* 25; compare *Scorpiace* 12).

Now the privilege of this favor [that is, to go without dying] awaits those who at the coming of the Lord will be found in the flesh and will, because of the oppressions of the Antichrist's time, deserve by an instantaneous death that is accomplished through a sudden change [Tertullian's way of saying "translation"] to be qualified to join the rising saints, as he [Paul] writes to the Thessalonians (*On the Resurrection of the Flesh* 41).

Methodius and Commodianus

Much as Tertullian did a hundred or so years earlier, Methodius made the resurrection of Christians happen at the same time that nature is renewed after the tribulation for the millennial kingdom of Christ (*Discourse on the Resurrection* 1.8). Similarly again and in the mid-third century, Commodianus put the resurrection of Christians after Antichrist's reign, between the tribulation and the millennium (*Instructions* 44, 80).

Hippolytus

Earlier in the third century Hippolytus wrote,

Now concerning the tribulation of the persecution which is to fall on the church from the enemy [he has been speaking about the Antichrist and about the Antichrist's persecution of the saints and continues in the same vein] . . . . That refers to the 1,260 days (the half of the week) during which the tyrant is to reign and persecute the church (*Treatise on Christ and Antichrist* 60–61).

Then in chapters 62–67 Hippolytus quoted biblical passages extensively that describe the tribulation and Jesus' subsequent return (Daniel 11–12; Matthew 24; Luke 21; 2 Thessalonians 2; Revelation 20), tied these passages to the future experiences of the church, and equated the return of Jesus after the tribulation with Paul's description of the church's rapture in 1 Thessalonians 4.

Cyprian   Still in the third century, Cyprian discussed the coming persecution of Christians by the Antichrist (*Treatise* 11.12) and explained as follows the purpose of Jesus' describing the tribulation in the Olivet Discourse (Matt. 24–25; Mark 13; Luke 21): "With the exhortation of his foreseeing word, instructing and teaching and preparing and strengthening the people of his church for all endurance of things to come . . ." (*Treatise* 7). Further, "the day of affliction has begun to hang over our heads, and the end of the world and the time of the Antichrist to draw near, so that we must all stand prepared for the battle. . . . A severer and a fiercer fight is now threatening" (*Epistle* 55.1). And yet further, "Antichrist is coming, but above and beyond him comes Christ also" (*Epistle* 55.7).

The Constitutions of the Holy Apostles   *The Constitutions of the Holy Apostles* 7.2.31–32 borrowed terminology from Paul's description of the rapture in 1 Thessalonians 4:16–17 (among other passages) and used it for Christ's coming after the tribulation to destroy the Antichrist (called "the deceiver of the world, the enemy of the truth, the prince of lies"), and also told Christians to endure throughout the tribulation as they watch for the Lord to come:

> Watch out for your life. "Your waists are to be belted, and your lamps burning, and you like those who are waiting for their Lord, when he will come, at evening or in the morning or at cockcrowing or at midnight. For at an hour that they do not expect, the Lord will come. And if they open to him, blessed are those servants, because they were found watching" [at this point a prominent pretribulationist again breaks off the quotation to make it seem as though the passage teaches that Christ may return at any moment and therefore before the tribulation] . . . for through the abounding of iniquity the love of many will grow cold. For people will hate and persecute and betray one another. And then will appear the deceiver of the world, the enemy of the truth, the prince of lies, whom the Lord Jesus "will destroy with the spirit of his mouth, who takes away the wicked with his lips. And many will be offended at him. But those who endure to the end, they will be saved. And then will appear the sign of the Son of man in heaven." And afterwards there will be the sound of a trumpet [blown] by the archangel, and in that interval there will be the revival of those who were sleeping. And then the Lord will come, and all his saints with him. . . .

Victorinus

Victorinus wrote the first known commentary on the Book of Revelation. The church's presence during the tribulation forms the basis of his entire commentary. Take one example: "He [John the author of

Revelation] is speaking about Elijah the prophet, who is the precursor of the times of Antichrist, for the restoration and establishment of churches from the great and intolerable persecution [followed by a lengthy discussion of the persecution of the church by the Antichrist]" (*Commentary on the Apocalypse* 7:2).

Lactantius

In the first part of the fourth century, Lactantius encouraged Christians to stand firm throughout the last times, which he described in terms of the plagues of the tribulation, persecution by the Antichrist, the coming of Christ and resurrection after the tribulation, the millennium, and the last judgment (*Institutes* 7.15–27; compare *Epitome* 71–72).

Athanasius and Cyril, Chrysostom and Augustine

So much for the first two or three hundred years following the New Testament period. There's nothing to be quoted for anyone's holding the pretrib view—or even arguing against it. Why not? It didn't exist. Nobody had thought it up. Our treatment of succeeding centuries can hop, skip, and jump. Approvingly, Athanasius cited the Christian prayer, ". . . they have not spared your servants, but are preparing the way for Antichrist" (*History of the Arians* 8.79). Cyril of Jerusalem taught, "The church . . . declares to you the things concerning Antichrist before they arrive. . . . it is good that by knowing these things, you should make yourself secure beforehand" (*Catechetical Lectures* 15.9). Chrysostom preached, ". . . the time of Antichrist . . . will be a sign of Christ's coming . . ." (*Homilies on First Thessalonians* 9). Augustine wrote, "But the one who reads this passage [Daniel 12] even half asleep cannot fail to see that the Antichrist's kingdom will fiercely, though for a short time, attack the church" (*The City of God* 20.23).

The Venerable Bede spoke of "the Antichrist and his war against the church" (*Explanation of the Apocalypse* [93:154 in Migne]). Bernard of Clairvaux said,

Bede and Bernard, Luther and Calvin

> Nothing remains but for the necessity that the demon of noonday appear in our midst to seduce those who still abide in Christ, who remain faithful to his truth . . . he ["the demon of noonday"] is even confident that he will devour the humble and the simple who are still in the church. For he is the Antichrist, . . . who "exalts himself against every so-called god or object of worship [2 Thess. 2:4]" (*Sermon on the Song of Songs* 33.16).

Martin Luther said that the Book of Revelation is a description "especially of tribulations and disasters that were to come upon Christendom [later, 'the Christians']" (*Preface to the Revelation of St. John II;* see also Luther's *Sermon on John 16:13*). John Calvin wrote of the Antichrist's pride as proceeding "to a public desolation of the church" (*Institutes* 4.7.25). And so on down to the present day.

At the same time, other opinions on the meaning of biblical prophecy were undergoing change. Most importantly, the thousand years or millennium of Christ's rule was shifted from its original position just following Jesus' return to the present age of the church. As time wore on, of course, the thousand years had then to be interpreted as symbolic of a period longer than a thousand years literally understood. And for a

The Stability of Posttribulationism in the Midst of Change

while the Book of Revelation came to be regarded as predicting the whole course of church history rather than concentrating on the end of that history. Despite such changes, however, the expectation remained steady that Antichrist comes first, only then the Christ.

The Evolution of Pretribulationism

Until the nineteenth century, or late eighteenth century at the earliest. Then, but not till then, the idea of a pretrib coming of Christ and rapture of the church arose and gained popularity in certain circles, especially of English-speaking Christianity and especially in the first half of the twentieth century. As mentioned before, there's a fair amount of agreement among those who've investigated the history of this teaching that its popular form developed more or less gradually, that it took a little time to reach the stage of mature pretribulationism: seven years of future tribulation, a coming of Jesus to take all true Christians (not just the best ones) out of the world for that period of time, and a coming of Jesus with them after the tribulation.

But investigators disagree among themselves over the question, Who was first to divide the second coming in two, put some time in between, and have the church taken out of the world in the first half of the second coming? And perhaps more importantly, who was it whose interpretations of this sort were adopted, developed, and popularized by others? Was it Morgan Edwards, a Welshman and Baptist who moved to America? Was it Manuel de Lacunza, a Roman Catholic who wrote in Spanish but whose writings were then translated into English? Or Edward Irving, a London preacher whose followers turned into a splinter group called the Catholic Apostolic Church? Or Margaret Macdonald, a Scottish teenager who claimed to have received a revelation concerning the second coming? Or John Nelson Darby, an Irishman and a founder of the movement known as the Plymouth Brethren, perhaps with the help of some of his cohorts? In a book of the present kind it's enough to say that whoever or however many came up with the theory of pretribulationism, they didn't do so till very, very late in the history of Christian teaching.

Naturally, teachers of pretribulationism try to minimize this historical embarrassment. On the one hand, they emphasize their appeal to the Bible itself as distinct from the history of Christian belief about biblical teaching. Fair enough, but we're talking perspective, not proof. On the other hand, they try to find in early Christian writings, if not a developed pretribulationism, at least the makings of pretribulationism in elements such as watchful expectancy for the return of Christ. Trouble is, the strongest statements of such expectancy are coupled with equally strong statements of expecting to meet the Antichrist first, in the future, just as in the New Testament itself; and throughout ancient Greek literature, we have seen, the terms used for expectancy do not at all have to imply the possibility of happening at any moment.

No to Incipient Pretribulationism

On yet another hand, teachers of pretribulationism appeal to "the progress of doctrine," that is, the development of Christian beliefs through increased understanding of God's Word in relation to historical and

No to Pretrib Progress of Doctrine

cultural conditions. Examples: The Bible doesn't use the language of Trinity—three persons in one, one person in three—but Christian theologians developed such language to explain biblical teaching about God in a way meaningful for their own time. The Bible doesn't use the language of orthodox Christology—two unmixed natures, human and divine, in the one person Jesus of Nazareth—but again, Christian theologians developed such language to refine biblical teaching about him in a way meaningful for their own time. Right within the Bible, too, you can see progress of doctrine. The Old Testament prophets didn't see a distinction between the first and second comings of the Messiah, but the New Testament makes the distinction. So why isn't it legitimate for us, having progressed beyond the understanding of earlier generations of Christians, to make a distinction between pre- and posttrib stages of the second coming?

But the New Testament writers who distinguished between the first and second comings were inspired. Teachers of pretribulationism aren't, so they have to produce convincing evidence from the Bible. Yet they haven't. And you'll notice that progress in Christian doctrine comes by way of developing what's already present in the Bible. For example, the division of Messiah's coming into two comings arose out of the incompatibility between suffering and triumph already present in messianic prophecies of the Old Testament (Isaiah 9, 11, and 53 being representative). You can't find any such incompatibility in prophecies about the second coming, however, nor can you find pretribulationism as such lying dormant in the New Testament. Wherever you look you find roadblocks that belie any notion of progress in the development of pretribulationism. Remember, for every possibility of progress there's a possibility of regress. Both Scripture and the history of Christian doctrine consign pretribulationism to the latter category.

Sometimes it's argued back that teaching about the second coming was so immature in the early church, and that other questions of Christian belief were so pressing— we've already mentioned God as Trinity, Christ as fully human and fully divine both at the same time and without a split personality, but there were also the doctrines of salvation by faith, not by works, of the church, reformed but one, and so on—well, it just took a long time for theologians to get around to developing the doctrine of Jesus' return. Wrong. It simply isn't accurate to describe as immature the early church's teaching about Jesus' return.

No to Pretrib Immaturity

The writings of Irenaeus, Hippolytus, and Lactantius confront us with full and challenging discussions concerning Daniel's seventieth week, the 1,260 days, the abomination of desolation, the ten toes and the mixture of iron and clay in Daniel's image, the ten horns, the little horn, the Antichrist, the false prophet, the apostasy, the reappearance of Elijah, restoration of worship in the Jewish temple, the significance of 666, comparisons of Daniel and Revelation, Babylon, Armageddon, the first resurrection, the rapture, the second advent, millennial conditions, the final resurrection, and the last judgment. The only significant

No to a Loss of Pretribulationism

matter that early theologians didn't develop appears to have been a pretrib rapture!

Again, it is sometimes argued that pretribulationism might have been lost for a long time just as the doctrine of justification by faith, or salvation by grace, was lost for a long time—till its rediscovery in the Protestant Reformation. But though that doctrine did grow dim, it wasn't lost. Just read *The Epistle to Diognetus* 8:6, "And he [God] manifested himself through faith, by which alone it is allowed a person to see God," or 9:3–5, "For what other than that one's [Christ's] righteousness could cover our sins? In whom was it possible for us the lawless and ungodly to be justified other than in the Son of God alone?" or the writings of Augustine against Pelagius, such as *On Grace and Free Will*, ". . . grace is not rendered to works but is given freely. . . . Why then do those very vain and perverse Pelagians say that the law is the grace of God by which we are helped not to sin?" (chapters 19, 23).

By contrast, pretribulationism doesn't appear at all in early Christian literature, or in any other Christian literature until recent times. Furthermore, the New Testament categorically affirms justification by faith, but does not likewise affirm a coming of Jesus before the tribulation to take the church out of the world. So this attempt at an argument from analogy doesn't work.

A Posttrib Recap

Wrapping it up: the perspective of history casts a long shadow over the novel belief in a pretrib rapture. The Bible, particularly the New Testament, turns out the lights on that belief by presenting only one return of Christ—after the tribulation. By presenting that return as the hope of the church in writings addressed to Christians. By telling Christians to watch for the Day of the Lord and then denying that that day will come before the tribulational career of the Antichrist. By linking the most extensive exhortations to watch for the second coming with Christ's coming immediately after the tribulation. And by saying that the events of the tribulation will signal the nearness of Jesus' return. Before those events, "the end is not yet" and the Christ is not yet "at the doors." *First the Antichrist!*

Clement of Rome

The late first-century *1 Clement* 23 spoke of the Lord's coming "speedily" and "suddenly," but we shouldn't deduce a pretrib coming from that statement. For Clement of Rome's language came in part from Malachi 3:1, in whose context Elijah's coming is said to precede the Lord's coming (compare 4:5–6). And Clement himself used the analogy of a tree's budding, putting forth leaves, and producing ripe fruit—very like the budding fig tree that Jesus used as an analogy for seeing the events of the tribulation as signals of his near return. So look eagerly; but look correctly, sensibly, biblically.

Pseudo-Ephraem

Recently, two passages in a sermon of Pseudo-Ephraem have been cited to prove an early date for belief in a pretrib rapture. Pseudo-Ephraem lived sometime during the late fourth century through the early seventh century and got a false identification with Ephraem the Syrian, a church leader of the fourth century. It seems that Pseudo-Ephraem borrowed some of his material from true Ephraem. The cited passages talk about Christians' meeting the Lord, his drawing them from the confusion that overwhelms the world, apparently during the tribulation, and about their being gathered before the tribulation and taken to the Lord.

Questions for a Postscript

But does Pseudo-Ephraem elsewhere put the meeting of Christians with the Lord before or after the tribulation? Does this meeting coincide and equate with Christians' being gathered and taken to the Lord before the tribulation, or does it follow the tribulation and therefore differ from being gathered and taken to the Lord? Do being gathered and taken to the Lord equate with a rapture of the church yet to happen before the tribulation, or to another kind of activity that is already taking place? What does being gathered and taken to the Lord mean in the Ephraemic tradition on which Pseudo-Ephraem draws? Does being drawn from the world's confusion mean or entail being taken out of the world itself, or does it mean to be delivered from confusion while remaining in the world? The correct answers to these questions will show Pseudo-Ephraem to have advocated posttribulationism, not pretribulationism. For those answers read the following Postscript.

Postscript

Pseudo-Ephraem
on Pretrib Preparation
for a Posttrib Meeting with the Lord

Pseudo-Ephraem's Sermon

On pages 306–17 of its July/September issue in 1995, the journal *Bibliotheca Sacra* carried an article under the title, "The Rapture and an Early Medieval Citation." Timothy J. Demy and Thomas D. Ice wrote the article. In it they cite a sermon of Pseudo-Ephraem, *On the Last Times, the Antichrist, and the End of the World,* as evidence for belief in a pretrib rapture of the church, a belief already current in the late fourth through early seventh centuries (the date of Pseudo-Ephraem being a matter of some doubt).[1] Though in his sermon Pseudo-Ephraem seems to regard the tribulation as three and a half years in length, not a full seven years, his dividing the second coming into two stages separated by a definite period of years called "the tribulation" would put the essential elements of pretribulationism cen-

---

[1]Ephraem is also spelled "Ephraim" and "Ephrem."

turies and centuries before the late eighteenth or early nineteenth century, the time to which the beginning of explicit
pretribulationism is usually assigned. But despite the widespread heralding of this "discovery," Pseudo-Ephraem's sermon and the interpretation given it by Demy and Ice require
another look.

A Pretrib Gathering

The particular passages given a pretrib interpretation appear in Section 2 of the sermon and read as follows according to Cameron Rhoades' English translation, used by Demy
and Ice and based on a Latin text:[2]

> Why therefore do we not reject every care of earthly actions
> and prepare ourselves for the meeting of the Lord Christ, so
> that He may draw us from the confusion which overwhelms
> all the world? . . . For all the saints and elect of God are gath-
> ered, prior to the tribulation that is to come, and are taken to
> the Lord lest they ever[3] see the confusion that is to overwhelm
> the world because of our sins.

Demy and Ice themselves offer the following translation of
what they describe as "the majority Greek reading" of "the
Greek variants of the proto-rapture passage in the sermon":

---

[2]For Cameron Rhoades' English translation and its Latin base, see *On the
Last Times, the Antichrist, and the End of the World: A Sermon by Pseudo-
Ephraem (written about A.D. 374–627)* (Washington, D.C.: The Pre-Trib
Research Center, n.d.). The present article will follow this translation except
where it needs correction or stylistic improvement. For easier understanding
of quotations taken from Pseudo-Ephraem's sermon and comparable patristic
literature, pronouns referring to deity will be capitalized.

[3]The version of Rhoades' translation published by The Pre-Trib Research
Center lacks "ever," which I have added for the Latin *quando*. But the version
published by Grant R. Jeffrey in "A Pretrib Rapture Statement in the Early
Medieval Church," *When the Trumpet Sounds,* ed. Thomas Ice and Timothy
Demy (Eugene, Oreg.: Harvest House, 1995), 111, has "at any time," an
equivalent of my "ever."

The elect ones are gathered together before the tribulation in
order that they might not see the confusion and the great tribulation which is coming upon the unrighteous world.[4]

Actually, C. P. Caspari, in whose edition the Greek as well
as the Latin is found, lists the Greek, not as a variant of
Pseudo-Ephraem, but as part of the genuine work of Ephraem
the Syrian, a church father of the fourth century, and as evidence for Pseudo-Ephraem's using the works of true Ephraem
in addition to those of others. And in addition to the truly
Ephraemic Greek source, Caspari also presents a truly
Ephraemic Latin source.[5] In fact, he cites several other truly
Ephraemic texts, both in Greek and in Latin, as sources for
this very passage in Pseudo-Ephraem's sermon.[6] With other
experts in the field, Paul J. Alexander, whom Demy and Ice
cite approvingly, refers to Caspari's presentation of these truly
Ephraemic materials and calls Pseudo-Ephraem's sermon a
pastiche of existing works.[7] It is therefore surprising that
Demy and Ice describe the Greek text as a variant of Pseudo-
Ephraem's sermon rather than taking advantage of the Greek
and other Latin texts as representative of true Ephraem's
works, and thus pushing the purported pretribulationism
back to him.

[4]Demy and Ice, "The Rapture and an Early Medieval Citation," p. 316,
note 45: οἱ ἐκλεκτοὶ συνάγονται πρὸ τῆς θλίψεως (πρὸ θλίψεως) τοῦ μὴ ἰδεῖν
τὴν σύγχυσιν καὶ τὴν θλῖψιν τὴν μεγάλην τὴν ἐρχομένην (μεγάλην ἐρχομένην)
εἰς τὸν ἄδικον κόσμον (τὸν κόσμον τὸν ἄδικον). This Greek text lacks the
element of being taken to the Lord.

[5]_Briefe, Abhandlungen und Predigten aus den zwei letzten Jahrhunderten
des kirchlichen Alterthums und dem Anfang des Mittelalters_, ed. C. P. Caspari
(Christiania [Oslo]: Mallingsche Buchdruckerei, 1890; reprint Bruxelles:
Culture et Civilisation, 1964), 445–52, especially 447; see also 208–20 for the
Latin text of Pseudo-Ephraem's sermon and, for a select but up-to-date
bibliography of Ephraem's works and of secondary literature on him and
them, _St. Ephrem the Syrian: Selected Prose Works_, trans. Edward G. Matthews
Jr. and Joseph P. Amar; ed. Kathleen McVey; The Fathers of the Church 91
(Washington, D.C.: The Catholic University of America Press, 1994), xv–xxx.

[6]_Briefe, Abhandlungen und Predigten_, pp. 446–47.

[7]Paul J. Alexander, _The Byzantine Apocalyptic Tradition_ (Berkeley/Los
Angeles/London: University of California Press, 1985), 17, 143, 147.

Omissions

But the pretrib interpretation of the two slightly separated passages in Pseudo-Ephraem's sermon runs into problems both elsewhere in that sermon and in the works of true Ephraem. (Here we would do well to remember the interpretative rule of context.) In the first place and significantly by pretrib standards, neither of the slightly separated passages cited for early pretribulationism mentions a coming of the Lord (as in the classic New Testament description of the rapture at 1 Thess. 4:16–17), or a resurrection of deceased Christians and translation of living ones (as in 1 Cor. 15:51–52; see again 1 Thess. 4:16–17 for the resurrection), or a heavenly destination (as in a pretrib understanding of John 14:2–4 and, often, of Rev. 4:1–2).

Unburied Christian Corpses

In the second place, to understand the gathering of all the saints and elect of God prior to the coming tribulation, and likewise their being taken to the Lord to escape the world's tribulational confusion, as removal from the earth at a coming of Christ before the tribulation—this is to make the passage contradict a statement in Section 4 of the sermon: "In those days people will not be buried, neither Christian, nor heretic, neither Jew, nor pagan, . . ." (compare the "constant persecutions" that will take place "when . . . the end of the world comes," according to Section 3; the "fleeing from the face of the serpent" by those who "bend their knees to God, just as lambs to the adders [*sic,* 'udders' for the Latin *ubera*[8]] of their mothers, being sustained by the salvation of the Lord, and while wandering in states of desertion they eat herbs," according to Section 8 in reminiscence of Rev. 12:6, 13–17, which concerns the tribulation; and "the righteous" on whom

---

[8]The translation reads correctly in Jeffrey's version (p. 114), but not in that of The Pre-Trib Research Center (compare note 3 above).

"this inevitability" will come "so that they may be found good by their Lord," and whom "the prophets Enoch and Elijah" will "call back" to be "faithful witnesses to God," rescued "from his [the serpent's] seduction," according to Section 9 in reminiscence of Revelation 11 and 13). The text distinguishes these Christian corpses from those of heretics as well as from those of Jews and pagans. Therefore we should think of true Christians, not of those belonging to an apostate church left out of a pretrib rapture.

During the Great Tribulation

And what are "those days" during which the corpses of Christians will lie unburied? Section 4 describes the days as a time of "intolerable pressure" (compare "the great tribulation" in Section 8), when "the earth is agitated by the nations" (wording reminiscent of Jesus' phrase describing the state of affairs just before his posttrib coming: "and on the earth agitation among nations" [Luke 21:25]). Again, the same section describes "those days" as a time when "people will hide themselves from the wars, in the mountains and rocks, by caves and caverns of the earth [phraseology reminiscent of the sixth seal, opened during the tribulation: '. . . they hid themselves in the caves and the rocks of the mountains' (Rev. 6:15)], . . . because there is nowhere to flee . . . . because the world will be overwhelmed by worthless nations, whose aspect appears to be that of wild animals more than that of a human being [compare the tribulational beasts of Revelation 13]."

When Antichrist Rules

These descriptions, it would be agreed on all sides, point to "the tribulation that is to come" (Section 2). So also do Pseudo-Ephraem's having said already that "the end of the world is near [compare Section 2: 'the end of the world is at hand, . . . it is the very last hour (*hora*, for which Rhoades has "time") . . . . it is the eleventh hour, and the end of the world comes to the harvest'], the consummation remains . . . . the coming of the Evil One [an apparent reference to 'the Antichrist,' as he is called in Section 10] is at hand" (Section 1), having said already that "there is nothing else which remains [to be 'fulfilled (consummated)'] except the advent of the Evil One[9] in the completion of the Roman kingdom" (Section 2), and having said already that the coming of the end of the world will be accompanied by "diverse wars, commotions on all sides, horrible earthquakes, perturbations of nations, tempests throughout the lands, plagues, famine, drought throughout the thoroughfares, great danger throughout the sea and dry land, constant persecutions, slaughters and massacres everywhere [and so on—a laundry list of those disasters that will fill the tribulation according to Revelation 6–18; compare relevant passages in the Olivet Discourse of Matthew 24–25; Mark 13; Luke 21]."

With Deception

Sections 5–10 add even greater specificity in describing this "great tribulation" of "three and a half years," "forty-two months," or "1,260 days," especially with regard to the activities of "the Antichrist," "that worthless and abominable dragon," "a young whelp of a lion *not* as the lion of the tribe of Judah" (italics added), "that abominable, lying, and murderous one . . . born from the tribe of Dan [the tribe omitted in the list at Rev. 7:5–8, and said in Judges 17–18 to have been the first Israelite tribe guilty of idolatry on entrance into Canaan]," "that abominable corrupter," "a wolf . . . concealed under the appearance of a lamb, . . . a greedy man . . . under the skin of a sheep," "the very wicked serpent," "the very fierce dragon," "the antagonistic serpent" and "son of perdition," "the enemy" who has "Satan" as "his

[9]Rhoades has "the wicked one" here, but the Latin is the same as in Section 1, where Rhoades puts "the Evil One."

father." The Antichrist's activities include deception, rebuilding of God's temple in Jerusalem, restoration to "the Jews" of "the practice of the first covenant," sitting "as God" in the temple, ordering "all nations" to worship him (compare 2 Thess. 2:3–5), and requiring "the serpentine sign on the forehead or on the hand" for the selling or buying of grain (compare "the mark of the Beast" in Rev. 13:16–18). And it is during this time that "God . . . sends . . . the prophets Enoch and Elijah . . . for the heralding of the second coming of Christ" (compare the prophesying of God's two witnesses for forty-two months of the tribulation according to Rev. 11:1–13).

At World's End

That the description of "those days" in Section 4 during which Christians lie unburied links up with descriptions of the tribulation in foregoing and following sections is supported by parallelism. Section 3 begins, "When therefore *(Cum ergo)* the end of the world comes, there arise diverse wars, commotions on all sides, horrible earthquakes, perturbations of nations, ..." Section 4 begins, "Whenever therefore *(Cumque igitur)* the earth is agitated by the nations, people will hide themselves from the wars in the mountains and rocks, ..." Section 5 begins, "Whenever *(Cumque)* the days of the times of those nations have been fulfilled, after they have destroyed the earth, ..." Section 6 begins, "When therefore *(Cum ergo)* the end of the world comes, that abominable, lying, and murderous one is born from the tribe of Dan." Section 7 begins, "But when *(Sed cum)* the time of the abomination of his desolation begins to approach, ..." The sections are obviously talking about the same period of time. There is no reasonable doubt, then, that "those days" in which the corpses of Christians lie unburied consist of the great tribulation, the time of Antichrist's rule.

Corpus Delicti

But what are the corpses of Christians doing there if according to the supposedly pretrib passages in Section 2 all Christians will have been gathered and taken to the Lord by means of a rapture that occurred before the tribulation—a rapture, moreover, that entailed the resurrection of all deceased Christians and thus left none of their corpses to lie unburied during the tribulation? A pretrib interpretation might posit a distinction between "all the saints and elect of God" as those who make up the church to be raptured before the tribulation, and "Christian" as describing those who become believers after a pretrib rapture of the church. But the text of Pseudo-Ephraem's sermon uses "saints," "elect," "Christian," "righteous ones," and "faithful witnesses to God" without specifying a terminological distinction between different groups of believers; and it would be the reverse of the usual pretrib view to make "saints" and "elect" refer to members of the church as distinguished from "Christian" in description of nonchurchly, tribulational believers. Furthermore, a parallel Greek text listed by Caspari as truly Ephraemic uses "saints" for those whom the Antichrist persecutes during the tribulation;[10] and "Christian" is a term regularly used in the New Testament and other literature for a member of the church. It therefore remains a problem for the pretrib interpretation of the sermon that Pseudo-Ephraem speaks of Christians as lying unburied during the tribulation, "the three and a half years" called "the time of the Antichrist" at the completion of which ("And when the three and a half years have been completed") "the Lord will appear with great power and much majesty . . . . and the Lord will destroy him [the Antichrist] by the spirit of His mouth. And he [the Antichrist] will be bound and plunged into the abyss of everlasting fire with his father Satan" (Section 10, drawing on the phraseology of 2 Thess. 2:8; Rev. 19:20; 20:1–3, 10, all in refer-

---

[10]*Briefe, Abhandlungen und Predigten,* p. 451.

ence—as again all sides would agree—to what will happen after the tribulation).

Posttrib Resurrection

The pretrib interpretation runs into another problem. Section 10 of Pseudo-Ephraem's sermon also says that the Lord will appear "with all the powers of the heavens, with the whole chorus of the saints, with those who bear the sign of the holy cross upon their shoulders, as the angelic trumpet precedes Him, ..." Thus far, one might think that the Lord's posttrib coming *with* the saints presupposes, and therefore implies, a pretrib coming *for* them, on which occasion they were raised from the dead, translated, and raptured. But the text goes right on to say that the angelic trumpet "will sound and declare: 'Arise, O sleeping ones [compare the Christians lying unburied during the tribulation in Section 4; also the Greek text listed by Caspari as truly Ephraemic[11]], arise, meet Christ, because his hour of judgment has come! Then Christ will come and the enemy will be thrown into confusion, and the Lord will destroy him by the spirit of His mouth . . . . but the righteous ones will inherit everlasting life with the Lord forever and ever [compare Paul's statement, 'And so shall we ever be with the Lord,' at the tail end of a description of the rapture (1 Thess. 4:17)]." Thus the resurrection of the saints, or righteous, is said to occur at the Lord's coming after the tribulation to destroy the Antichrist; and where their resurrection is, there also is their rapture. Hence, the coming for the saints and the coming with them merge into one: the Lord comes with and for them on the same occasion—with their departed spirits (as in 1 Thess. 4:14; compare the disembodied souls of martyrs under the heavenly altar in Rev. 6:9–11), for their resurrected bodies and the translated living, and with all of them together in continued descent.

[11]Ibid., p. 452.

Posttrib Meeting

A further problem for the pretrib interpretation of Pseudo-Ephraem's sermon arises out of this same and final Section 10. The deceased righteous are told not only to "arise" but also to "meet Christ." The Latin verb translated "meet," *occurrite* (more literally translated "run to" or "hasten to"), is cognate to the Latin noun *occursum*, "meeting," in the supposedly pretrib passage of Section 2: ". . . prepare ourselves for the meeting of the Lord Christ." Since Section 10 explicitly and indubitably puts this meeting after the tribulation, the parallelism of terminology with Section 2—and also with the phrase "for a meeting of the Lord in air" in Paul's description of the rapture (1 Thess. 4:17, translated literally)—indicates that Pseudo-Ephraem sees the meeting in Section 2 as occurring after the tribulation and therefore as differing from the saints' being gathered and taken to the Lord "prior to the tribulation" according to a slightly later passage in Section 2.

The Imminence of Antichrist's Coming

In confirmation of a posttrib placement of the meeting is the discussion presented in Section 1 and the first part of Section 2. There, though "the coming (advent) of the Lord is near," "the consummation remains" and the end of the world cannot come until "the completion of the Roman Empire," which completion requires "the advent of the Evil One [that is, the Antichrist]." Sections 6–7 describe the way in which "he takes the empire." But his advent "remains"—it lies yet in the future—and it is all that remains before the Lord's coming and the saints' meeting with the Lord take place: ". . . there is nothing else which remains, except the advent of the Evil One in the completion of the Roman kingdom" (Section 2). So what is imminent, according to Pseudo-Ephraem, is not the Lord's coming and our meeting him,[12] but the Antichrist's advent

[12]Against Demy and Ice, "The Rapture and an Early Medieval Citation," p. 317; Thomas Ice, "Examining an Ancient Pre-Trib Rapture Statement," *Pre-Trib Perspectives* 2/2 (April 1995): 2.

with the tribulational events that it entails (compare Section 5: ". . . then the consummation comes, when the kingdom of the Romans begins to be fulfilled, and all dominions and powers have been fulfilled," the consummation itself completing the breakup of the Roman Empire that will have already begun according to Section 1: "In those days two brothers will come to the Roman Empire who will rule with one mind; but because one will surpass the other, there will be a schism between them. And so the Adversary will be loosed and stir up hatred between the Persian and Roman empires. In those days many will rise up against Rome; the Jewish people will be her adversaries"—all prior to "the advent of the Evil One ['Antichrist']," when he "takes [or 'receives'] the kingdom [or 'empire']" (Sections 6–7; compare also Section 2: "incursions of the barbarians").[13] It is also notable that Section 10 puts the *post*trib coming of the Lord "in the hour which the world does not know, and on the day which the enemy, or[14] son of perdition, does not know," and that Section 9 puts the Lord's finding the righteous "good" also at the posttrib coming.

The Lord's Empire

Furthermore, immediately following the call to "prepare ourselves for the meeting of the Lord Christ," Pseudo-Ephraem announces that "the coming (advent) of the Lord is near," that "the end of the world is at hand," and that "it is the very last hour." These three parallel statements link up naturally with Christians' meeting the Lord. Since in Section 2 "the end of the world" leads directly to "the empire of the Lord," which hardly arrives before the Antichrist's tribulational rule, Christians' meeting the Lord at the end of the

---

[13]The question of Pseudo-Ephraem's engaging in "prophecy after the event," and if so, to what historical events he was referring, need not occupy us. We are concerned only with his presentation of a prophetic chronology, however much or little of it was truly future to him.

[14]The version of The Pre-Trib Research Center has "of" instead of "or." The Latin has *uel,* meaning "or" in the sense "that is, i.e." Again, Jeffrey's version is correct (p. 114; compare note 3 above).

world must occur according to Pseudo-Ephraem at the Lord's posttrib coming (compare the tribulational descriptions of "the end of the world" in Sections 3 and 6). It may also be noted that this meeting draws on the background of Jesus' triumphal entry, at which Jerusalemites went out to meet him and escort him back into their city (John 12:12–13), as would happen at a posttrib rapture (compare the statement in a tradition of true Ephraem, "Arise, go out to meet Him with Hosannas . . ." [*A Hymn Against the Jews Delivered on Palm Sunday* 16]).[15]

[15]Here and below, references in the body of the text to true Ephraem's works are supplemented in notes with references to some available English translations of those works. This first translation comes from J. B. Morris, *Select Works of S. Ephrem the Syrian* (Oxford: John Henry Parker/London: F. and J. Rivington, 1847), 75. Others will come also from Sebastian Brock, *The Harp of the Spirit,* Studies Supplementary to Sobornost 4 (San Bernadino, Calif.: Borgo, 1984); Henry Burgess, *The Repentance of Nineveh* (London: Robert B. Blackader, 1853); idem, *Select Metrical Hymns and Homilies of Ephraem Syrus* (London: Robert B. Blackader, 1853); John Gwynn, "Selections Translated into English from the Hymns and Homilies of Ephraim the Syrian," *A Select Library of the Nicene and Post-Nicene Fathers of the Christian Church,* Second Series, ed. Philip Schaff and Henry Wace (New York: Charles Scribner's Sons, 1905), vol. 13, part 2, pp. 113–341; Carmel McCarthy, *Saint Ephrem's Commentary on Tatian's Diatessaron,* Journal of Semitic Studies Supplement 2 (Oxford: Oxford University Press on Behalf of the University of Manchester, 1993); Kathleen McVey, *Ephrem the Syrian: Hymns,* Classics of Western Spirituality (New York: Paulist, 1989); Robert Murray, "St Ephrem the Syrian on Church Unity," *Eastern Churches Quarterly* 15 (1963): 164–76; and Robert Murray, *Symbols of Church and Kingdom: A Study in Syriac Traditions* (Cambridge: Cambridge University Press, 1975). At times I have updated and corrected the English style of these translations. In one passage "gather" has substituted for "assemble" because of their synonymity. And occasionally I have had to supply my own translations into English. The abbreviation CSCO refers to Corpus Scriptorum Christianorum Orientalium, published in Louvain during recent decades by Secrétariat du CorpusSCO. The addition of SS refers to Scriptores Syri, a Syriac series forming part of the larger Oriental series and containing works of Ephraem edited and translated into German by Edmund Beck. The addition of SA refers similarly to Scriptores Armeniaci, an Armenian series also forming part of the larger Oriental series and containing Ephraemic material edited and translated into English by George A. Egan. The first number following these abbreviations represents the volume number in the

From Pseudo- to True Ephraem

Within Pseudo-Ephraem's sermon, then, Christians lie un-buried during the tribulation. They are raised from the dead, meet the Lord, and are found good by him not until his coming after the tribulation, so that their "meeting of the Lord Christ" in the first supposedly pretrib passage of Section 2 can hardly refer to a pretrib meeting without contradicting a good deal else in the sermon. Since Pseudo-Ephraem draws from the tradition of true Ephraem, as Demy and Ice themselves acknowledge, indeed emphasize,[16] a further and extensive look at that tradition may offer some additional guidelines for understanding Pseudo-Ephraem's sermon. The guidelines turn out to be post- rather than pretrib.

Our Enemy the Antichrist

According to the tradition of true Ephraem, "there is nothing still remaining except that the coming of our enemy the

Oriental series as a whole, the second number that of the Syriac or Armenian series. In line with references to English translations, I have referenced only the volumes of German translation in CSCOSS. Individually preceding volumes in the series contain Ephraem's Syriac. References to Assemani have to do with the old edition of Ephraem's works in Greek, Syriac, and Latin: *Sancti Patris Nostri Ephraem Syri Opera Omnia*, ed. Josephi Simonii Assemani (Rome: The Vatican, 1737–43), vols. 1–6. Compare note 5 above. Experts doubt the authenticity of some of the works cited as Ephraemic. Hence the references to tradition as well as to Ephraem himself. Even those works which as a whole may not come directly from him may nevertheless encase authentically Ephraemic material. No attempt will be made here to decide these questions. For our purposes it is enough that the materials attributed to Ephraem belong to the background providing a context for the interpretation of Pseudo-Ephraem's sermon.

[16]Demy and Ice, "The Rapture and an Early Medieval Citation," p. 312: "Caspari and Alexander have demonstrated that Pseudo-Ephraem was 'heavily influenced by the genuine works of Ephraem'" (quoting and citing Paul J. Alexander, "The Diffusion of Byzantine Apocalypses in the Medieval West and the Beginnings of Joachimism," *Prophecy and Millenarianism: Essays in Honour of Marjorie Reeves*, ed. Ann Williams (Essex, UK: Longman, 1980], 59; see also Ice, "Examining an Ancient Pre-Trib Rapture Statement," p. 2).

Antichrist be revealed" (*Sermon on Asceticism*).[17] Ephraem warns "us" Christians against the Antichrist because the Antichrist will come before the Christ (*Sermon on the End and the Consummation, the Judgment and the Reward, and on Gog and Magog, and on the False Messiah* 433–40).[18] Likewise, ". . . the tribulation will be upon us . . . the dawn of the morning will be near to us for the good news and joy of our Lord; as also our Savior said, . . . 'For the sake of the elect those days will be shortened'" (Ephraem, *An Exposition of the Gospel* 91).[19] "Therefore before the rise of the Man of Wickedness, we must teach and admonish people (about) his ways, and his deceits. . . . Even our Savior said, . . . 'If possible, he ["the Man of Wickedness"] would lead astray many of the elect'" (ibid. 93).[20] This passage goes on to describe as our hope the coming of Christ after the tribulation (ibid. 94).[21]

Then in terms reminiscent of 2 Thessalonians 2:1–12, Ephraem returns to warning Christians against being deceived by "the Man of Sin" (ibid. 99),[22] applies to his Christian audience Jesus' descriptions of the great tribulation in the Olivet Discourse (ibid. 100),[23] denies that prophecies concerning the abomination of desolation and destruction of Jerusalem and the temple were exhausted by the events of A.D. 70, and avers that Jesus spoke his command to flee to the mountains "concerning His church" (ibid. 101).[24] "That great tribulation . . . approaches and comes upon us" (ibid. 102).[25] So "let us be watchful . . . for the manifestation (and) coming of the sedition [of the Antichrist; see 2 Thess. 2:1–4] which is to be revealed on the earth" (ibid. 114)[26] and "get ready to oppose that one who is armed . . . with diverse means and de-

[17]Assemani, vol. 1, p. 44.
[18]CSCOSS 321/139, p. 91.
[19]CSCOSA 292/6, p. 68.
[20]CSCOSA 292/6, p. 69.
[21]CSCOSA 292/6, pp. 69–70.
[22]CSCOSA 292/6, pp. 73–74.
[23]CSCOSA 292/6, p. 74.
[24]CSCOSA 292/6, p. 75.
[25]CSCOSA 292/6, p. 76.
[26]CSCOSA 292/6, p. 114.

ceits, with signs and miracles of his powers, to frighten us suddenly with very great temptations" (ibid. 115).[27] No wonder that Ephraem envisions "our labors and endurement of great tribulation" (ibid. 119).[28] Such quotations could be multiplied indefinitely out of his *Exposition of the Gospel*. Elsewhere he also puts the gathering of resurrected saints at the Lord's coming in power and glory and judgment, that is, at the posttrib coming, just as Pseudo-Ephraem does (Ephraem, *On Magicians, Sorcerers, and Soothsayers, and on the End of the World* 277–80, 333–44).[29]

Future Meeting

Since the last-mentioned sermon of Ephraem uses "gathering" for the posttrib resurrection of saints, the question now arises, What does Pseudo-Ephraem mean by his statement, "For all the saints and elect of God are gathered, prior to the tribulation that is to come, and are taken to the Lord lest they see the confusion that is to overwhelm the world because of our sins" (Section 2)? Obviously, this gathering, occurring as it does before the tribulation, cannot equate with the gathering of Christians in resurrection after the tribulation. And we noted earlier that the pretrib gathering cannot equate with "the meeting of the Lord Christ" (Section 2), for that meeting is later put at the resurrection following the tribulation (Section 10).

Present Gathering

Let us first observe the use of the present tense of the verbs of gathering (*colliguntur* both in Section 2 of Pseudo-Ephraem's Latin sermon and in that sermon's Latin Ephraemic source;[30] συνάγονται in the Greek Ephraemic

[27]CSCOSA 292/6, p. 84.
[28]CSCOSA 292/6, p. 87.
[29]CSCOSS 321/139, pp. 17–19, 25, 27, 71, 94.
[30]For the Latin Ephraemic source, see *Briefe, Abhandlungen und Predigten*, p. 447.

source[31]) and of taking (*adsumuntur* both in Section 2 of Pseudo-Ephraem's Latin sermon and in that sermon's Latin Ephraemic source[32]). Of course, the present tense is often used in a futuristic sense, as elsewhere in Pseudo-Ephraem's sermon. Section 1 provides an example: "Whenever the Roman Empire has begun to be consumed by the sword, the coming of the Evil one *is at hand* [Latin: *adest*—present tense]. . . . In those days two brothers will come [followed by a string of further verbs in the future tense, so that 'is at hand' must mean 'will be at hand']."

But more frequent than a futuristic use of the present tense is its use for an action or state of being in progress. As every student of Greek and Latin knows, this use is often translated best into English by a form of the verb *to be* plus an -ing form. Thus, a likely better translation of the second passage under contention in Section 2 reads as follows: "For all the saints and elect of God *are being gathered* prior to the tribulation that is to come, and *are being taken* to the Lord lest they ever see the confusion that is to overwhelm the world because of our sins." This understanding is favored not only by the greater frequency of the progressive present tense, but also by the contrast between meeting the Lord Christ after the tribulation, and being gathered and taken to the Lord before the tribulation.

Gathering as Evangelism and Conversion

To what might a being gathered and taken to the Lord that is going on right now refer? Answer: to being evangelistically gathered and taken to the Lord in Christian conversion.[33] And favoring this answer is an abundance of evidence in the Ephraemic tradition on which Pseudo-Ephraem draws:

---

[31]Ibid.

[32]Ibid.

[33]Compare the American evangelical lingo of "bringing people to Christ." If stress falls on "all" in Pseudo-Ephraem's statement that "all the saints and elect of God are being gathered and taken to the Lord prior to the tribulation

"Because the sons of Jerusalem are dispersed and scattered among all the nations of the Gentiles, learn who he is who has reunited and *gathered* all the nations of the Gentiles into the Church" (Ephraem, *Commentary on Tatian's Diatessaron* 20.29).[34] "For the Gentiles the Church was built, a *gathering* for prayers" (*Saint Ephraem's Hymn Preserved in Armenian* 48.13–24).[35] "For it was fitting that our Lord be the haven of all good things, unto whom [people] might be *gathered* together, the end of all mysteries, towards whom they would hasten from everywhere, . . ." (*Commentary on Tatian's Diatessaron* 1.1).[36] "For You [O Lord] *gather* from everywhere the rebellious children of Adam" (*Hymn on the Death of a Private Person*).[37]

"Learn therefore, O Hebrew [unbelieving Jew], that the Lord has built Jerusalem . . . . saying to her, '. . . as you are bereaved of Israel, because I have removed him from My side, I will open your gates with joy and the hosts of the Gentiles will enter you and will become in you an elect people [cf. 'elect of God' in Pseudo-Ephraem's sermon] . . ." (*A Hymn Against the Jews Delivered on Palm Sunday* 20).[38] There follows a passage which borrows the language of Old Testament prophecies concerning the restoration of Jerusalem and indicates the present fulfilment of those prophecies in the church—often in the future tense because of the Old Testament standpoint: "Because Jerusalem was vexed at the cry of the children's voices [at Jesus' triumphal entry in Matt. 21:15–17], the church will *gather* in children, and they will praise Me with their Hosannahs. And as she [the church] invited the

---

that is to come," the statement may exhibit an expectation that nobody will be converted during the tribulation: the full complement of elect ones will have been reached beforehand. But "all" may refer to those elect who are at the present time being gathered, without regard to the elect who have already been gathered and will yet be gathered, whether during the tribulation or in the meantime.

[34]McCarthy, p. 308; Murray, p. 64.

[35]Ibid., p. 79, citing *Patrologia Orientalis*, vol. 30, p. 222.

[36]McCarthy, pp. 39–40.

[37]Burgess, *Hymns and Homilies*, p. 15, citing Assemani, vol. 6, p. 275. Literally translated from Syriac, the last phrase reads "the rebellion of Adam."

[38]Morris, p. 77.

children to glorify Me in the streets, I will *gather* to her the multitude of the nations [the influx of believing Gentiles into the church], and they will chant to Me with Hosannahs. And Jerusalem and her children [here, figures for the church and her members] will cry out, 'Blessed is He Who has come [a reference to Jesus' first advent] and is to come [a reference to the second advent, so that the gathering has to do with evangelism and conversions at present, that is, between the two advents, not with the streaming of nations to Jerusalem in a millennial kingdom following the second advent]'" (ibid. 20).[39]

The foregoing statements are to be set against the background of Ephraem's comments on the gathering at Jesus' entry into Jerusalem: "and there were *gathered* the children and prophets with disciples that they might bring in the King with pomp and with the grandeur of their Hosannahs. The church of the Gentiles longed for Him and worshipped Him, . . ." (ibid. 12;[40] compare the statement, "The church and her ministers, the city and its dwellers, will give praise for Your salvation"—*Nisibene Hymn* 4.28[41]). Also displaying Ephraem's exposition of present fulfilment in the church are the following passages: "Blessed be He Who chose for Himself a holy church, and behold, she praises Him with Hosannahs" (*A Hymn Against the Jews Delivered on Palm Sunday* 25),[42] and "the saints ['are joyful for a sinner when he returns from his crimes to repentance'] in the midst of their assemblies [that is, gatherings]" (*An Exhortation to Repentance* 4.34).[43]

Yet further statements elaborate this churchly fulfilment in greater detail. For example, "Exult and rejoice, you daughter of Jerusalem; for behold, your King comes riding . . . . Arise, give praise, you holy church, and receive the Bridegroom with Hosannahs, and with infants and children sing praises among the nations on the festive day of our Redeemer, Who has come and delivered you from error." "The people

[39]Ibid.
[40]Ibid., p. 69.
[41]Gwynn, p. 173.
[42]Morris, p. 82.
[43]Burgess, *Repentance*, p. 179.

['Israel'] is exchanged for the nations [later, 'the church']" (*A Hymn Against the Jews Delivered on Palm Sunday* 19–20).[44] "Whatever both Prophets, Isaiah, and Ezekiel have said about the delivery and restitution of the Jews is to be taken of the days of the [first] coming of our Lord and of the preaching of His Gospel" *(Commentary on Isaiah)*.[45]

In a noneschatological passage, one dealing with the present state of the church, Ephraem calls the Lord "the *Gatherer* of all [Christian believers]" (*Hymn Concerning the Faith [contra Scrutatores]* 1.22).[46] "He Who is to be worshipped came down to His birth and *gathered* worship to Himself. Blessed is He Who is worshipped by all" (*Hymn on the Nativity* 22.15;[47] compare *Hymn for the Feast of the Epiphany* 14.49, "All you peoples, come and worship Him,"[48] and 15.5, ". . . that the peoples should come and exult in the Great Light that has come down to earth"[49]). "This is He Who flew and came down from on high. And when all those gifts [later described as people with 'a lowly and humble soul' and as those who 'receive (Christ)'] . . . saw Him, . . . they *gathered* themselves together from every side to come and be grafted into their natural tree . . . . namely, to the Godhead, Who in sufficiency came down to the people of Israel that the parts of Him might be *gathered* to Him" (*Sermon on Our Lord* 57, 59;[50] again compare Pseudo-Ephraem's phraseology of being "*gathered* and taken to the Lord"). There follows a reference to the similar ingrafting of Gentile believers (ibid. 58).[51]

"His [Christ's] voice rent the graves and rent the sanctuary. It scattered the nation of crucifiers [unbelieving Jews] and *gathered* the nations [the multinational church, especially Gen-

---

[44]Morris, p. 76.

[45]Ibid., p. 73, note d.

[46]Ibid., p. 375.

[47]CSCOSS 187/83, p. 101; McVey, p. 182; alternatively numbered 15.15 in Gwynn, p. 253.

[48]Ibid., p. 286.

[49]Ibid., p. 287.

[50]CSCOSS 271/117, pp. 53–54; alternatively numbered 55, 57 in Gwynn, pp. 329–30.

[51]CSCOSS 271/117, p. 54; alternatively numbered 56 in Gwynn, p. 330.

tile believers]; and they believed in His deity and confessed the very God, the Son of very God" (*Hymn on the Faith [adversus Scrutatores]* 63.1).[52] "That from all churches there may be a single Church of truth; and let her children be *gathered, righteous* in her bosom, that we may confess Your goodness" (ibid. 52.15).[53] "I [the Lord] will call the nations *to me* [compare this phraseology and 'the Church has come *to our Lord*' (*Commentary on Tatian's Diatessaron* 11.4[54]) with 'are being taken *to the Lord*' in Pseudo-Ephraem's sermon]. And in the midst of Zion I will place a choice stone, one of stumbling; and the person who trusts on his name *will not be confused*, says the Lord [compare *'lest they ever see the confusion* that is to overwhelm the world' in Pseudo-Ephraem's sermon]" (*A Hymn Against the Jews Delivered on Palm Sunday* 19).[55]

"May the Lord of heaven rain down His blessings on our calamities, and His consolations on our afflictions, and His *gathering* on our dispersion" (*Nisibene Hymn* 21.20).[56] "Praised be He Who has *gathered* the divided peoples, so that they have become an indivisible people" (*Hymn on the Fasting for Forty Days* 5.4).[57] "All the nations that have believed in Him and by Him . . . have been *gathered* into the one house, which is the Church" (*Commentary on Zechariah*).[58] "Lord, let Your truth *gather* Your children under my wings" (*Nisibene Hymn* 29.4).[59]

Ephraem calls Jesus "the Humble One [compare Matt. 21:5, quoting Zech. 9:9] Who *gathered* her chicks [compare Matt. 23:37]" and goes on to draw a parallel with the pilgrimages of Christians from all nations to Jerusalem: "Better for you [Jerusalem] . . . that instead of that people which was

[52]Morris, p. 318.

[53]Murray, "St Ephrem the Syrian on Church Unity," p. 175; idem, *Symbols of Church and Kingdom*, p. 149.

[54]Ibid., p. 137.

[55]Morris, p. 76.

[56]Gwynn, p. 193.

[57]CSCOSS 247/107, p. 11.

[58]Murray, *Symbols of Church and Kingdom*, p. 227.

[59]Murray, "St Ephrem the Syrian on Church Unity," p. 172; idem, *Symbols of Church and Kingdom*, p. 149.

uprooted [unbelieving Israel] from all peoples they [present-day Christians] should come with Hallelujahs to see in your wombs the [empty] grave and Golgotha" (*Hymn Against Julian* 4.21, 25).[60] "I have seen you scattered; I have seen you *gathered*" (*Hymn on Julian Saba* 24.8–10, 12).[61] "Bring back those who are without, and make those glad who are within. Mighty is Your grace, which You extend within and without. Let the wings of Your grace *gather* my chicks . . . . Bring home those of mine who are far off. Make glad those of mine who are near. And in the midst of our land will be preached good tidings of joy" (*Nisibene Hymn* 6.28, 33).[62]

"*Gather* and come [to Jesus the Great Physician, according to context], O lepers, and receive purification without labor" (*Hymn on the Nativity* 12).[63] "He [Christ] confines the day [in context, the Sabbath] to *gather* the wandering [in context, miracles of healing as a gathering of sinners to salvation]" (*Hymn on Virginity* 35.4).[64] "Behold, Jesus *is gathering* multitudes; but as for me [Death, personified, is speaking], in His feast a fast is being proclaimed for me" (*Nisibene Hymn* 35.6).[65] "The sea crowns You [the Lord] by the catch it offers You . . . It *gathered* and heaped the net of the apostles with a symbol of one hundred fifty fish [compare John 21:1–14]" (*Hymn on Virginity* 33.8).[66] This theme of Christ's gathering Christian believers to himself attains so much force that Ephraem even makes the Antichrist imitate that gathering with one of his own: "Like a partridge he [Antichrist] will *gather* to himself the sons of confusion" (on Jer. 17:11;[67] so also *Sermon on the End and the Consummation, the Judgment and the Reward, and on Gog and Magog, and on the False Messiah* 441–44).[68]

[60]McVey, pp. 25, 27.

[61]Murray, *Symbols of Church and Kingdom*, p. 93.

[62]Gwynn, p. 176.

[63]Ibid., p. 247; Morris, p. 55.

[64]McVey, p. 417.

[65]Gwynn, p. 194.

[66]McVey, p. 409; compare Brock, p. 51.

[67]See Alexander, *The Byzantine Apocalyptic Tradition*, p. 141.

[68]CSCOSS 321/139, p. 92.

"To the feast full of wise meanings you have been invited,
my beloved. Offer the gifts of praise to the Wise One Who invited you. To the marriage supper of all noble things you have
gathered yourselves, . . ." (*A Hymn Against the Jews Delivered
on Palm Sunday* 1).[69] "It [the greeting 'Peace!' in its sense of
salvation] was being sown in all houses so that it might *gather*
in [all] its members" (*Commentary on Tatian's Diatessaron*
8.4).[70] "When you [the pearl of Christian faith[71]] came up from
the sea, that living tomb, you cried out, 'Let me have a goodly
gathering of brothers, relatives, and kinsmen' . . . . for people
have loved and seized and adorned themselves with you as
they did with that Offspring with Whom the Gentiles loved
and crowned themselves [that is, with Christ]" (*The Pearl* 2.1).[72]
"He [the Lord] took and set him [Abraham bishop of Nisibis]
as a mind in the midst of the great body of the church, and his
members *came around him* [that is, *gathered*] to buy from him
life, doctrine, new bread" (*Nisibene Hymn* 17.3).[73] Ephraem
speaks about "the wheat it ['a breath of the Holy Spirit'] *is gathering* into the granary of life that has no tares [a reference in
context to the separation presently taking place between orthodox Christians and heretics]" (*Hymn on the Faith [adver-
sus Scrutatores]* 38.4;[74] contrast the church's being "scattered"
because of heresy and malpractice in the *Hymn Concerning
the Faith [contra Scrutatores]* 3.23).[75] "Since the Second Adam
is a body that came from there ['Paradise'], the hungry eagles
gathered to Him. Through the spiritual bread, every person becomes an eagle that can attain to Paradise. The one who has
eaten the living bread will also fly on the clouds to Him" (*Hymn
on Unleavened Bread* 17.11–13).[76] Here, gathering to Christ to
eat of him represents present conversion and participation in

[69]Morris, p. 61.

[70]McCarthy, p. 147.

[71]See, for example, *The Pearl* 6.3: "they saw the jewel, even the faith"
(Morris, p. 100); also 4.3 (ibid., p. 95).

[72]Ibid., p. 90.

[73]Gwynn, p. 186.

[74]Morris, p. 227.

[75]Ibid., p. 415.

[76]CSCOSS 249/109, p. 26.

the Eucharist, and flying to him on the clouds after having eaten of him represents future rapture.

In view of the foregoing evidence, it seems an understatement to say that Ephraem and his tradition make heavy use of Jewish pilgrimages to Jerusalem as a symbol of all nations' being gathered evangelistically and taken to the Lord in Christian conversion.[77] This use is neither obscure nor rare. It is clear and frequent, and it appears throughout a wide range of his writings. We have every right, then—indeed, every obligation—to apply the use to Pseudo-Ephraem's sermon, drawing as it does on Ephraem's works and those attributed to him.

By contrast with this use of being gathered and taken to the Lord for Christian conversion at the present time, the only eschatological use of gathering that I have been able to discover in Ephraem's writings has to do with the aforementioned gathering of followers by the Antichrist and gathering of resurrected saints at Jesus' coming after the tribulation, plus the gatherings of all people to the last judgment and of wicked people into Gehenna, and the final "gathering" of the Lord's name to the Lord himself: "They [angels] will gather together our unhappy race before the judgment seat" *(A Prayer in Prospect of Judgment);*[78] "And they [angels] will collect together the dust of Adam . . . they [human beings] will come to judgment" *(Hymn for the Lord's Day);*[79] "Your day, Lord, will gather them ['the troublers'] into Gehenna" *(Nisibene Hymn* 56.23).[80] "Because, then, worship also was rendered to the Name by all the nations ['Gentiles'], at the last the worshipful Name will be gathered in entirely to Its Lord" *(Sermon on Our Lord* 8).[81] That is to say, a gathering of saints in rapture at a pretrib coming of Jesus seems missing elsewhere

[77]"Symbol" (more literally translated from the Syriac as "mystery") is a favorite word of Ephraem. It appears time after time in his writings. As a poet (nearly all his writings consist of poetry), he naturally gravitated to symbols.

[78]Burgess, *Hymns and Homilies,* p. 64, citing Assemani, vol. 6, p. 484.

[79]Burgess, *Hymns and Homilies,* p. 83, citing Assemani, vol. 6, p. 499.

[80]Gwynn, p. 210.

[81]Ibid., p. 308.

in the Ephraemic tradition, whereas that tradition presents a tribulational gathering and several kinds of posttrib gatherings, including one of resurrected saints, and contains an avalanche of references to present gathering in the taking of converts to the Lord through Christian evangelism.

The Danger of Confusion

Pseudo-Ephraem states the purpose of the present gathering and taking to the Lord: "lest they ['all the saints and elect of God'] ever see the confusion that is to overwhelm the world because of our sins" (Section 2). "Overwhelms" stands for *obruet,* present tense, which Rhoades correctly takes as futuristic (though earlier he translated *obruet* with "overwhelms"—Section 2). Being gathered and taken to the Lord at the present time has the purpose of not seeing (in the sense of not experiencing) confusion at a future time. This purpose is the same as that for which we Christians are to "reject every care of earthly actions and prepare ourselves for the meeting of the Lord Christ," namely, "so that He may draw us from the confusion which overwhelms all the world" (Section 2). Conceivably, the drawing from confusion provides the purpose for Christians' *meeting* the Lord. But the hortatory thrust of the question, "Why therefore do we not reject every care . . . and prepare ourselves . . . ?" favors a purpose for the *rejection* and *self- preparation.* So our present rejection of care and our present preparation to meet the Lord Christ have the purpose of drawing us from future confusion.

At the Consummation

When will that confusion arrive? When "the consummation comes" and "that worthless and abominable dragon will appear," "leaping from Basan," which "is certainly interpreted as 'confusion,'" that is to say, "in the last day . . . . When therefore the end of the world comes" and "that abominable, lying, and murderous one is born from the tribe of Dan [compare other ancient tradition that the Antichrist will come from that tribe[82]] . . . . when the time of the abomination of his desolation begins to approach" and "he orders the temple of God to be rebuilt for himself, which is in Jerusalem," so that "after coming into it, he will sit as God and order that he be adored by all nations . . . . Because the very wicked serpent will direct every worship to himself . . . . and there will be a great tribulation" (Sections 5–8, excerpts). Obviously, Pseudo-Ephraem is pointing to the reign of Antichrist during a future tribulation: the language echoes the tribulational passages Daniel 9:27; Matthew 24:15–22; Mark 13:14–20; 2 Thessalonians 2:3–4.

Craftiness

Where will that confusion come from? It will come from the Antichrist's "iniquity" and "lying" as "the crafty dragon" who "has the appearance of righteousness." He will be "craftily gentle to all people, not receiving gifts [that is, not taking bribes], not placed before another person [not at first putting himself forward], loving to all people, mild to everyone, not desiring gifts, appearing friendly among close friends, so that people may bless him, saying, 'He is a righteous man,' not knowing that a wolf lies concealed under the appearance of a lamb, . . ." (Sections 5–6). Even "the righteous, . . . the faithful witnesses" will stand in danger of "his seduction" (Section 9).

Seduction

What will that confusion consist of? It will consist of a seduction so crafty that "the Jews will congratulate him [the Antichrist], because he gave them again the practice of the first covenant," and "then all people from everywhere will flock together to him at the city of Jerusalem," where "he will sit as God and order that he be adored by all nations" (Sec-

---

[82]Irenaeus, *Against Heresies* 5.30.2; Hippolytus, *Treatise on Christ and Antichrist* 14.

tion 7).[83] But the one true God will turn the tables on Antichrist by confusing the confuser himself through sending a "consolatory proclamation" in the mouths of "the prophets Enoch and Elijah, who, while not tasting death, are servants for heralding the Second Coming of Christ, and in order to accuse the enemy. And when those just ones [Enoch and Elijah, singled out from the righteous ones in general] have appeared, they confuse indeed the antagonistic serpent" (Section 9). "Then Christ will come, and the enemy will be thrown into confusion" (Section 10).

Enoch and Elijah

What is the effect of Enoch's and Elijah's consolatory proclamation? The effect is that they "call back the faithful witnesses [the rest of 'the righteous'] to God in order to [rescue them[84]] from his [the Antichrist's] seduction" (Section 9; compare the Greek text listed by Caspari as truly Ephraemic[85] and indicating that Enoch and Elijah will cry out, "He [the Antichrist] is a deceiver . . . . No one should believe him at all," so that people will "not believe the tyrant on account of

---

[83]For the motif of confusion in the writings of true Ephraem, see *Hymn on Virginity* 40.12 (McVey, p. 435); *Hymn on the Faith (adversus Scrutatores)* 67.2 (Morris, p. 326); *Hymn Concerning the Faith (contra Scrutatores)* 3.3, 7 (ibid., pp. 404, 408); *Nisibene Hymns* 6.17; 36.15 (Gwynn, pp. 175, 197); and, above all, *Sermon on the End and the Consummation, the Judgment and the Reward, and on Gog and Magog, and on the False Messiah* (CSCOSS 321/139, pp. 89–93), where Ephraem expatiates on the Antichrist and the confusion caused by him.

[84]Rhoades supplies "free them" instead of "rescue them," but freeing would imply prior enslavement to the Antichrist's seduction, and such enslavement would probably contradict the designation "the righteous ones" (alternatively, "the just ones"—Rhoades uses both translations for *iusti*). The idea seems to be that the ministry of Enoch and Elijah is needed to call back the righteous from getting caught in the web of Antichrist's seduction. Jeffrey's version of Rhoades' translation fails to bracket "free from" as supplied (p. 114), but the version of The Pre-Trib Research Center correctly brackets the phrase (compare note 3 above). As implied, the Latin text has nothing at this point.

[85]*Briefe, Abhandlungen und Predigten*, p. 451.

fear"). A further effect is that "the righteous will inherit eternal life with the Lord forever and ever" (Section 10).

The Rest of the Righteous

And who are these righteous ones, these faithful witnesses, whom Enoch and Elijah call back to God during the tribulation so as to make them inherit eternal life at the coming of Christ after the tribulation, more particularly, "when the three and a half years have been completed, the time of the Antichrist," and the Lord Christ "will destroy him by the spirit of His mouth"? They are those who "arise" to "meet Christ" (Section 10). Once again, then, a later section puts the purportedly pretrib "meeting of the Lord Christ" (Section 2) at the posttrib coming of Christ. Since that meeting draws "us" at the completion of the tribulation from the tribulational confusion which overwhelms all the world (Section 2 again), the drawing cannot equate with being gathered and taken to the Lord. The latter actions are being done "prior to the tribulation that is to come" (Section 2 yet again).

Rescue from Confusion

So the present gathering and taking to the Lord prepare the elect of God lest they ever experience the confusion that leads "the unrighteous" to worship the Antichrist. As evangelism, in other words, these actions turn "the elect" into "the righteous." The ministry of Enoch and Elijah will then call the righteous back to God when the Antichrist's seduction lures them during the tribulation. (Pseudo-Ephraem may have deduced the need for such a call-back from Jesus' saying that during the tribulation, signs and wonders will be performed "to deceive, if possible, even the elect" [Matt. 24:24; compare Mark 13:22].) And the righteous meet Christ at his coming after the tribulation.[86] This posttrib meeting defines

[86]In dependence on Alexander, *The Byzantine Apocalyptic Tradition*, pp. 210–11, Demy and Ice understand Christians' being gathered and taken to the Lord as removal from the earth for the purpose of survival, and this

the rescue from the tribulation that a parallel Greek text listed by Caspari as truly Ephraemic[87] talks about: "that we may be rescued from (ῥυσθῶμεν ἐκ) the tribulation which is going to come on the earth." So also another parallel Greek text listed by Caspari as truly Ephraemic speaks of "the saints" as being "rescued from the dragon" who has been persecuting them to the point of their fleeing into the deserts and hiding themselves in the mountains and in caves and holes of the earth.[88]

The True Teaching of Pseudo-Ephraem

In summary, then, Pseudo-Ephraem urges Christians to forsake worldliness in preparation for meeting Christ when he returns after the great tribulation. Meanwhile, Christian evangelism is taking people to the Lord and gathering them into the Church. As a result of their present conversion and its confirmation by their preparation to meet Christ, he will save them from being sucked into the vortex of confusion that will overcome others likewise on earth throughout that period. This interpretation takes account of Pseudo-Ephraem's leaving the corpses of Christians unburied during the tribulation, putting the resurrection of Christians and their meeting Christ at his coming after the tribulation to destroy the Antichrist, making imminent the advent of Antichrist rather than that of Christ, and utilizing the plainly and heavily post-trib tradition of true Ephraem, who repeatedly portrayed present-day evangelism as a gathering.

---

removal, in turn, as a substitute for shortening the tribulation to three and a half years with the same purpose, the latter method being "the normal approach in other apocalyptic texts" ("The Rapture and an Early Medieval Citation," p. 316; see also Ice, "Examining an Ancient Pre-Trib Rapture Statement", p. 3). But Pseudo-Ephraem's seeing a tribulation of only three and a half years makes unnecessary a removal from the earth for the purpose of survival. The stated purpose of Christians' being gathered and taken to the Lord is to avoid "confusion," not to avoid extinction.

[87]*Briefe, Abhandlungen und Predigten,* p. 447.
[88]Ibid., p. 451.

Scripture Index

189

Subject Index

obert H. Gundry has taught the Bible to tens of thousands of students, both directly and indirectly, since becoming a professor in 1962. He has taught at Westmont College for thirty-five years, and he is the author of *A Survey of the New Testament*, a standard textbook used in many colleges since its publication in 1970. *Survey* is now in its third edition and has been translated into Portuguese, Korean, and Serbo-Croatian.

First the Antichrist is Gundry's second book on the end-times. His first, *The Church and the Tribulation* (1973), was more technical and has long been out of print.

Since obtaining his Ph.D. at the University of Manchester under the tutelage of F. F. Bruce, Gundry has established himself as a first-rate New Testament scholar. He has published two monographs and major commentaries on both Matthew and Mark. He has also had many articles appear in such periodicals as the *Journal of Biblical Literature, New Testament Studies,* and *Novum Testamentum.*

The high esteem in which Gundry is held by his colleagues became clear in 1994 with the publication of *To Tell the Mystery: Essays on New Testament Eschatology in Honor of Robert H. Gundry.* This appeared in the Journal for the Study of the New Testament Supplement Series, published by an academic publisher in Sheffield, England.